W9-DFP-582

DRIED FLOWER TECHNIQUES BOOK

Over 50 techniques for creating beautiful arrangements

Anne Ballard

NORTH LIGHT BOOKS
Cincinnati, Ohio

SOMERSET CO. LIBRARY
BRIDGEWATER, N.J. 08807

A QUARTO BOOK

First published in North America in 2001
by North Light Books,
an imprint of F&W Publications, Inc.,
1507 Dana Avenue
Cincinnati, OH 45207

Copyright © 2001 Quarto Inc.

All rights reserved. No part of this
publication may be reproduced, stored in a
retrieval system or transmitted in any form
or by any means, electronic, mechanical,
photocopying, recording or otherwise,
without the prior permission of the
copyright holder.

ISBN 1-58180-208-0

QUAR.DFAT

Conceived, designed, and produced by
Quarto Publishing plc
The Old Brewery
6 Blundell Street
London N7 9BH

Project Editor Nadia Naqib
Art Editor Sheila Volpe
Designer Tanya Devonshire-Jones
Assistant Art Director Penny Cobb
Photographer Pat Aithie
Copy editor Claire Waite
Proofreader Lynn Bresler
Indexer Diana Le Core

Art Director Moira Clinch
Publisher Piers Spence

Manufactured by Regent Publishing
Services Ltd, Hong Kong
Printed by Leefung-Asco Printers Ltd,
China

Contents

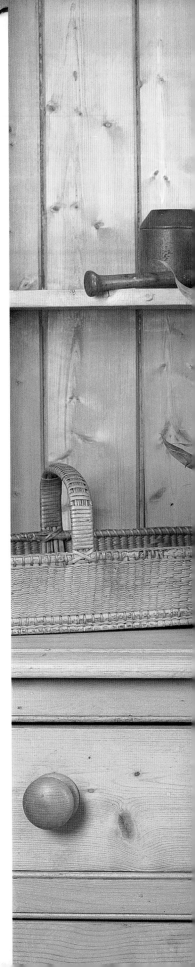

INTRODUCTION

My love of dried flower arranging has brought me many friendships, and hours of pleasure from growing, harvesting, drying, and arranging the sheer variety and versatility of plants available. Flowers and plants never cease to amaze and inspire, from the simplest herb to the most flamboyant peony—there is a home and design for all—and working with dried flowers can become a fascinating pastime or an absorbing career.

Dried flowers can bring any number of qualities to a home. They can brighten up a bedroom, add elegant warmth to a dining room, or bring rich texture and vibrant color to a kitchen. Try to stay abreast of trends in dried flower arranging and to adapt them to your own lifestyle and interior decor. Above all, find the time to enjoy making the arrangements of your choice, and have the courage to experiment.

You can begin experimenting simply by using the flowers in your garden. When pruning, collect twigs and leaves, gather seed heads, and take note of all the available flowers and plants that you could use to add style and interest to your home.

Tackle the techniques and projects in this book with an open mind, put away any rules you may have learnt from working with fresh flowers, and be prepared to get creative. I have referred to plant names throughout using a mixture of Latin and common names, for ease of reference. Whether you are a newcomer or an experienced dried flower arranger, this book will give you a wealth of ideas to design with. So let me share the secrets of this wonderful trade.

Look first to your garden to gather plants to choose for harvesting and drying.

A pine dresser provides a wonderful backdrop to this arrangement as it blends with the cones, while bringing out the colors of red and lime, and the sumptuous textures.

MATERIALS AND EQUIPMENT

Tracking down the necessary equipment for dried flower arranging should not be a problem as garden centers and craft shops have a huge range. Also try good florist stores, hardware shops, or use a specialist wholesaler (see pages 124–125).

Try to always keep your materials and tools close at hand so that you do not have to interrupt your work to search out essential pieces of equipment and spoil the flow of creativity.

Binding wire

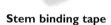

Garden twine

Cutting

Knife
Use a long kitchen knife for cutting through dry florist's foam blocks, and trimming dry florist's foam to shape. A craft knife with removable blades is useful for cutting woody stems on a diagonal angle. You can also use a knife to hold down materials during gluing, if the glue gun is particularly hot.

Saw
A saw is a useful accessory when cutting through tough stems, tree trunks, and branches to create topiary tree bases.

Wire cutters
You will need wire cutters to cut chicken wire.

Scissors

Pruning shears

Scissors
Floral scissors have a serrated inner edge that makes it easy to cut through tough stems, such as artichoke and *Protea*. Sharp dressmaker's scissors are used for trimming ribbons: they quickly become blunt if used for cutting stems.

Pruning shears
Pruning shears are spring-loaded cutters available in many sizes and strengths. They will cut through varying thicknesses of material. Find a pair you feel comfortable with. When in use always keep the blade uppermost and try making two or three cuts rather than fighting and wrenching at the material.

Binding

Binding wire
Binding wire on a reel is available in a range of gauges and metallic colors and is essential for making swags and garlands, and binding moss around basket edges. Colored wires are often used in headdresses and as decoration within a design. Remember that the higher the gauge the thinner the wire. Experiment with different thicknesses until you find one you are comfortable working with.

Garden twine
This string is particularly suitable to dried flower arranging since it is available in shades of brown and green that blend well with all dried materials. Use it to bind tied bunches to a wreath or garland, or as a decorative bow.

Raffia
Traditionally used by gardeners, this makes an attractive alternative binding material for a rustic finish, or as an alternative to ribbon.

Stem binding tape
This rubber-based tape is used for binding around wires to make a hanger, and neatening the unattractive ends of wired bunches.

Florist's wires
Florist's wires are available in different lengths and gauges and are used for mounting and bunching flower stems and foliage. It is best to use wire that is as thick as you can comfortably work with: the inexperienced hand sometimes finds this wire difficult to handle. The heavier the material, the thicker the wire you will need to hold it in place. Use silver rose wire for fine work.

Raffia

Florist's wires

Saw

Knife

Wire cutters

Stem binding tape

Dry florist's foam

Various mosses

Floral clay

Candle holders

Anchor tape

Mossing pins

Securing

Anchor tape
Narrow and shiny on one side, anchor tape sticks to dry florist's foam and is useful for holding it in position while you work, or for binding blocks of foam together.

Candle holders
These plastic fittings have a star-shaped base that is easily pushed into dry florist's foam to hold a candle. They are available in a range of sizes.

Floral clay
Floral clay is usually used to secure material to a base. Use it to secure a candlestick too large for a candle holder.

Stones/gravel
Stones or gravel can be used to balance a lightweight container or as a decoration.

Stones

Plaster of Paris
Available from most local craft suppliers, plaster of Paris makes a good base to set a topiary stem in. You can also use finishing plaster or cement for a cheaper alternative; however, they do take longer to set.

Useful extras

Canes, skewers, and cocktail sticks
These are useful for securing heavy items, such as candles and terracotta pots, into an arrangement, and to extend the length of a stem with the help of stem binding tape.

Clear sealer
A clear sealer is a very light varnish used as a clear fixative, designed especially for dried materials. It holds and lifts colors and keeps the material clean. Alternatively, artists' fixative can be used in the same way.

Florist's spray paints
Fashion moves quickly, and it is useful to keep a range of florist's spray paints, available in a host of colors, so you will always be ahead of the trends. These paints can be used on foliage, flowers, or containers to change, coordinate, or enhance the original colors.

Turntable
A turntable is a useful, though not essential, piece of equipment that enables you to work clearly above the usual worksurface.

The base

Dry florist's foam
Dry florist's foam forms the basis of most flower arrangements, into which individual stems, wired stems, or wired bunches are inserted. This foam is available in rectangular blocks, spheres, cones, and cylinders. Larger display blocks can also be purchased. Always use the gray or brown foam; the green foam is designed for use with fresh flowers and tends to crumble when used with dried material.

Gluing

Glue gun and glue stick
A glue gun with a trigger feed is the easiest form of glue to use for dried flower arranging. The gun heats sticks of clear glue to a very high temperature, and then squeezes it through a nozzle. The glue gun is an extremely useful tool for binding material together or adding an artificial stem.
    The glue gun can burn; so if it is in use for long periods, turn it off to cool periodically.

Glue gun

Moss and pins

Mosses are exceptionally useful in most dried flower arrangements. They are often used to cover and disguise the mechanics of a display, such as a block of dry florist's foam, a wreath ring, or a garland base made from chicken wire, and to fill in any small gaps in a finished piece.

Coco moss
This is an extremely useful moss that comes from the coconut and is available in a variety of dyed colors. It is useful to finish the top of a container, or as part of a design.

Reindeer moss
Reindeer moss is available in a wealth of dyed colors and hides a multitude of sins in any arrangement.

Sphagnum moss
The dried flower arranger could not survive without sphagnum moss. It covers dried florist's foam wherever it is used and makes a wonderful background on a wreath and for garlanding baskets.

Mossing pins
Ready-made mossing pins can be bought and used to keep moss in place on dry florist's foam. You can also make your own by bending 22-gauge florist's wire into a hairpin.

Glue sticks

Nylon reinforced plaster

Topiary and garlands

Chicken wire
You can find chicken wire suitable for topiary work and wall hangings in hardware or garden stores. Available in different gauges, it is also used for extra support around florist's foam to hold large stems such as artichokes. An alternative, plastic-coated wire, is available. Use pliers to twist chicken wire.

Nylon reinforced plaster
An easy to use plaster suitable for setting topiary bases into pots, or as a weight for displays where balance may be a problem, such as on a narrow shelf.

Chicken wire

Plaster of Paris

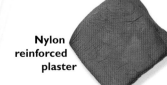

GETTING STARTED

Harvesting and preserving plants

Preserving your own much-loved garden plants and treasures can be great fun, and using your own dried materials in arrangements makes them all the more unique.

   Choose one of the drying techniques detailed on the following pages, select quality materials, cut at the right time, and enjoy drying and preserving flowers and foliage to bring pleasure throughout the year.

Harvesting

Knowing the correct stage at which to harvest materials comes with experience: some flowers are collected in bud, others in early flower, at a mature stage, or when a seed pod has developed. Harvesting is a science, so allow yourself plenty of time to study it.

   Only pick material to preserve when it is in perfect condition, since blemishes or fading will be emphasized during the drying process. Collect material in reasonably small bundles in dry weather, and dry as quickly as possible after picking.

Air drying

This is the simplest, most natural, and cheapest method of drying plant material. Don't be tempted to use a greenhouse or conservatory, garage or outhouse when air drying because bunches quickly fade and go moldy in these conditions. It is always disappointing to go to all the trouble of preserving your garden flowers to no avail.

   Choose a dry, airy, dark place and select bunches of material with woody stems, such as achillea, *Alchemilla*, and *Gypsophila*, as these dry more easily with this method than plants with fleshy stems. Tie the plants in bundles using a rubber band. The secret is to dry the

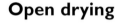

bunches as quickly as possible after they have been picked. Try not to make the bunches too compact, as the air cannot get to the central flowers. Hang the bundles on a horizontal rod or wire.

   If you have a large airing cupboard, or a dry area (perhaps over a boiler), you can hang the bunches here. Warm air speeds up the drying process, and helps to retain good color. If you have a dehumidifier it will help to extract the unwanted moisture.

Open drying

Heavy headed plants, such as *Zea mays* and alliums, can be dried on a chicken wire rack secured to a box.

Open drying heavy flower heads

Using glycerine

Glycerine is not a way of drying plants, rather a method of preserving them. Glycerine can be bought from drug stores, or supermarkets. This method is used predominantly for maintaining the suppleness of foliage. Good plant material to try would be heather, oak, beech, and eucalyptus. Thick leathery leaves such as fatsia respond best when totally immersed in the mix.

Pick the material in the height of summer, while the sap is still rising. Choose your material carefully, since you do not want to waste this expensive method on damaged or imperfect material. The quicker you can preserve the material after picking it the better as once wilted it is difficult to revive.

Mix two parts boiling water to one part glycerine, and pour into a narrow container: for tough, leathery leaves a 50:50 mix is recommended.

Smash the woody stems to make it easier for the mix to rise. Stand the stems in 3in (7cm) of the glycerine mixture, giving them plenty of room. Place the jar in a warm, dry atmosphere, away from other air drying projects. Most materials will take around three weeks to dry, and the container should be topped up with the glycerine and water mix as required.

The preserved material will last indefinitely and remain pliable. You will see a variety of color changes, and a slightly oily sheen when completed. A few drops of food coloring added to the glycerine solution changes the color ranges.

Water drying

This method of drying preserves the shape of the stem or flower head better than if the flowers were hung. Fill a container with 2in (5cm) of cold water. Remove excess foliage and arrange your flowers in the water so they do not touch each other, to allow good air circulation. Place in a dark, dry, and airy room. The water will evaporate and the plants will benefit from the slow drying process that results.

Water drying

Glycerine drying

Using desiccants

A desiccant is a fine-grained material which readily absorbs moisture. Using desiccants to dry material is quicker than air drying and this method much more readily retains the shape and color of the original plant. But it is a more elaborate and expensive method of drying. Stems also become very brittle as a result of this method of drying so plants have to be wired either prior to or after drying (see pages 12–13).

Silica gel, which is available in garden centers, drug stores, or hardware stores, is a useful desiccant to use for drying flowers with very delicate petals, such as pansy, zinnia, and anemone. Don't rush this delicate procedure.

Choose a sturdy box with a lid and spread a layer of silica gel in the container. Wire the flower heads (see pages 12–13).

Lay out the wired flower heads carefully in the box and trickle more silica gel over the top, remembering not to flatten the flowers: you want to finish up with a three-dimensional flower.

Use an artist's brush to build up the silica gel carefully to support the petals. Put on the box lid.

Leave to dry at about 82°F (28°C). Drying times vary depending on plant material, so periodically test after a few days. If the material is light and crisp it is ready. If soft, it is too dry and needs to be replaced: overdried material will only be suitable for pot pourri.

When dry, remove the flowers from the desiccant. Take care with delicate materials and use an artist's brush to ease the flowers out, and store in a lidded box. Don't pack too tightly—I use tissue—and keep in a dry atmosphere. Keep the silica gel for future use.

Microwave drying

Microwave ovens can be used to evaporate moisture in a flower or leaf and speed up the silica gel technique. Drying in a microwave without silica gel generally gives a very poor result.

Cover the bottom of a microwavable container with silica gel and arrange the unwired flower heads carefully on the gel. Cover with a thin layer of silica gel, avoiding squashing the flower.

Use a medium setting of about 300–350 watts, or start with a defrost at about 200 watts if you are unsure. Do experiment before trying your treasured plant. Times vary, but as a guide 2–2½ minutes for 10oz/250g is about normal. Be cautious, since you can always give a little longer if not dry: from experience I know it is easy to overcook. Leave to stand for about 15–30 minutes after drying before packing away.

Using silica gel

Microwave dried flower heads

Dried fruit

Pressed flowers

Drying fruit

Fruits are worth drying when in season. Oranges, lemons, limes, grapefruits, and blood oranges are easily sliced (not too thickly) and allowed to dry slowly, turning occasionally, in a very low oven, over a radiator, or in a warm airing cupboard.

Try cutting a whole tangerine or orange like a lantern, and allow to dry in the same way.

To dry apples, mix 1oz (30g) salt with 1 pint (500ml) water and soak slices of apple. Then thread the slices onto raffia and put to dry in a warm airing cupboard or over the boiler.

Pressing

Pressing is a quick and convenient method of preserving flowers. All material must be dry and free of blemishes. Pick only quantities of flowers you can deal with at once, as most suitable material will wilt quickly.

If you don't have a flower press, use sheets of newspaper or blotting paper. Place flowers singly on the paper and cover with more paper. Press between boards, a heavy rug, or a pile of books.

Leave for at least three weeks, then carefully remove and store between sheets of paper in a box. Pressed flowers are very delicate and need to be protected with self-adhesive film or glass. Try hellebore, pansy, ivy, or *Alchemilla mollis*.

Storing

Flowers must be absolutely bone dry to store.

Use tissue paper to line a lidded box and layer with dry flowers, the heaviest items at the bottom. Be very careful not to crush the flowers in the storage process.

Label the sealed box and store in a dry, dark area. Be aware of mice, especially where linseed, cereals, and poppies are stored. Peonies will benefit from storage with a mothball.

Keep silica gel dried flowers safely in an airtight container, remembering to label all storage boxes.

Storing dried flowers in tissue paper

Basic techniques

Before you begin to build up a dried flower arrangement, you need to be confident about some of the basic techniques, such as wiring plant materials into bunches or individually for stability and ease of use, preparing your containers, and making the finishing touches.

Wired flowers

Wiring

Wire is an essential dried flower arranger's tool that is available in various thicknesses and lengths. Use fine rose wire for delicate stems, fine medium gauge florist's wire for general use, and heavy gauge florist's wire for heavy construction work.

It is essential that you master the skill of wiring, since loose and untidy wiring leads to disappointing results.

Wiring leaves
Leaves are often bought with little or no stem, so this technique creates a stem to work with. Here we have taken an oak leaf from a branch to use singly in an arrangement.

Hold the leaf firmly with the back facing you. Thread the wire carefully behind the main vein, making a small, neat stitch.

Bring both ends of the wire down toward the stalk. Keeping one end straight, bind the other round the short leaf stem and second wire. Bring the two wire ends together to form a firm stalk.

Double leg wiring
Take a few stems of material and cut to the length required. Hold flowers in the palm of one hand. Put a florist's wire evenly behind the flowers

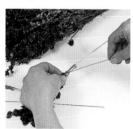

Wired lavender and a wired cone

and bring the two wire ends downward, either side of the stalks. The wire looks like a large hairpin with the loop supporting the bunch. Wind the bottom wire end firmly around the other wire end and the stalks a couple of times, bringing the wire down the stem as you go. You should now have a neat, firm bunch.

Center wiring
This is a useful basic skill for many designs. Collect a bunch of material together slightly fanned out and trim to the required length. Hold the flowers in the palm of your hand and put a florist's wire behind the bunch at the base of the flowers. Cross the two ends over and firmly twist the wires together to produce a strong support. Keep the wire ends at right angles to the bunch.

To wire bunches of twigs or cinnamon, use the center wiring technique with heavier florist's wire.

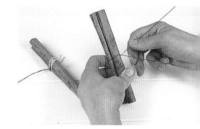

Trim the material to the required length. Fold the florist's wire centrally around the bunch. Cross over the two ends of the wire, firmly twisting them together and keeping the wire ends at right angles to the bunch. Cover with raffia, moss, or ribbon to disguise the wires.

Wiring a single flower head
Push a wire through the base of a flower head, keeping one end longer than the other. Bend both pieces of wire together, twisting the long end around the short one until secure. Then bend downward to make a new stalk.

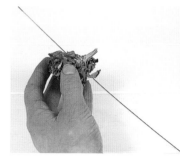

Alternatively, make a hole in the base of the flower and push a florist's wire through. Bend the top of the wire to form a hook and pull back until it is embedded in the flower head. Don't try this if your flower is very brittle.

Another method is to make a slight "V" shape in the bottom of the flower head, and choose a suitable replacement stem: if the flower has a short stem, choose a replacement stem with a cavity, like wheat, and thread the short stem into the cavity, gluing firmly in place with a glue gun.

It is also possible to glue a bent florist's wire to a flower head.

Wiring a corncob

Hold the head of a corncob firmly in the palm of your hand, stalk uppermost. Put a strong wire above the husk at the base of the cob, and twist the wires together firmly to make a strong stem. Change the position of the wires depending on how you need to use it.

Wiring cones

Cones often require wiring, and I like to use a cone wired up exactly where the stem was.

Hold the cone firmly. Thread a wire between the scales at the base of the cone, so it is hidden.

Take the wire ends halfway round the cone, and bring both ends under the base where the branch was originally attached. Twist the wires firmly together.

Wiring fruit slices

Take a medium gauge florist's wire to wire a single slice of fruit or a group of three or four slices. Hold the slices in a fan shape. Push the wire through the middle of the slices and twist together at the top.

Wiring a lantern fruit

Holding the fruit in one hand, push a wire through at the open slits near the base, so you have an even amount of wire on both sides.

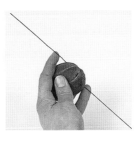

Cross the two ends and twist together at the base of the fruit to form a strong support.

Wiring a flower pot

There are two techniques you can choose from to wire a plant pot. Cut a piece of cane or twig the size of the base of the pot. Form a strong wire into a hairpin. Pin the cane or twig in the pot base with the two wire ends coming out through the bottom hole. Twist the wires firmly together at the pot base to secure.

Using a long, strong florist's wire, or two joined together if the pot is large, thread one of the wire ends through the pot

and over the top edge, keeping the wire tight to the pot inside and out. Twist the ends firmly together where they meet at the base.

Wiring a candle

With the aid of mossing pins, bent florist's wires, cocktail sticks, or wooden skewers, you should be able to give any candle "legs" that will firmly secure it in any design.

Always remember that the combination of candles and dried material is potentially dangerous. Never leave a display with a lighted candle burning unattended. Keep your material low and away from the candle where possible. Fire retardant sprays are available and worth sourcing—but still remember never to leave a lit display unattended.

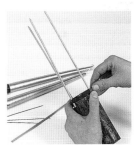

To prepare a candle, wrap anchor tape tightly around the base, but do not cut the tape. Place your choice of candle legs under the loose end of the tape, and tape firmly around the candle base, securing the legs as you go. The number of legs you need depends on the height and diameter of the candle. Finish by pulling the tape tightly round a couple more times and trim.

Guttering

At times it is necessary to neaten wired bunches with stem binding tape.

Wire up your material and select the most suitable color of stem binding tape. Hold the bunch in your left hand and wind a strip of tape at the top of the wire to secure. Holding the tape tightly in the right hand, keep it at a downward angle, and keep twisting the wire into the tape, bringing the tape down at the same angle until the wire is covered. Wrap firmly at the bottom so no wires show and cut the tape.

Preparing a container

Never underestimate the importance of getting the container correctly prepared: rushing on at this time often creates a disaster later.

Dry florist's foam
First make sure your chosen container stands evenly on a surface. Look at your container and trim a block of dry florist's foam with a knife to roughly the same shape. Push the trimmed foam into the container. Think about your planned design. Do you need the foam above the edges, or is the plant material actually inside the container? Use newspaper to raise the foam if necessary, so you can have material falling over the edges of the container.

You will soon learn to use less and less foam. If your container is deep, fill the whole of the base with newspaper. You then only need one block of foam on top. You will not always need foam at the edges of a container.

Basket with florist's foam

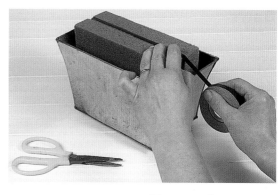

Always fix the foam very securely in place. The golden rule is never to start work on an arrangement unless the base is 100% safe. Wrap binding wire over the foam in a basket, or anchor tape over the foam in pots, vases, and ceramics—it can always be snipped off when *in situ*. If necessary, where the foam is difficult to secure, use a small piece of foam as a wedge, positioned much lower than the main block.

Mossing
Cover the foam with sphagnum moss to soften the arrangement, make it look natural, and to cut down on the amount of material used.

Pin sphagnum moss on very thinly with mossing pins or hairpins simply bent from florist's wire. If the moss is layered too thick, you may have problems inserting the stems, so cover thoroughly but thinly.

Preparing a hanger

A hanger is used to hang a wreath or garland from the wall. Hold a heavy florist's wire with anchor tape fixed on the top at a downward angle. Roll the wire into the tape so that it sticks. Twist the wire while holding the tape firm, until the wire is completely covered.

Bend the bound wire double and thread it into the weave on the back of your design, leaving a loop to hang from. Wind the ends of the wire together and through the wicker or metal until secure. Twist the loop a couple of times to make sure all is safe.

Bows

The preparation of a bow depends on the design to be trimmed and the width of the ribbon. The tail length again is a matter of personal choice.

It is always easier to use wired ribbon, although this is more expensive than unwired. However, with care, any ribbon can produce an attractive bow.

Leave a length of ribbon for one tail. Hold the ribbon between your thumb and forefinger and make a loop to the left, bringing the ribbon to the back. Gather loosely together and turn over the ribbon before repeating on the right.

Once you have two loops you have formed a single bow. At this point you can either twist a wire over the center to secure, and trim the tail end, or go on to form a double bow.

After forming the two loops of a single bow, continue in the same way to make two more. Always loop to the back and gather and turn.

Hold the center firmly and twist a wire over the center to secure.

The gathering makes the bow fuller, and remembering to always turn the ribbon means when working with a ribbon only decorated on one side, it is always seen at its best.

Cut a small strip of ribbon. Fold this over the center to neaten and glue at the back. This makes a knot in the center. You could use a contrasting ribbon in the center (or maybe raffia). Cut the second tail to the desired length neatly.

Tails

It can be useful to add tails separately to complete a design.

Divide a short length of ribbon in two, preferably not equal lengths. Gather and twist a wire at the chosen center.

Spray painting and gilding

After drying, materials can be treated with spray paints, varnish, and gilt creams. Florist's spray paints have become available in a kaleidoscope of colors. So as not to be wasteful, try to spray over a box containing a variety of plant material. If you are only using the heads then don't be generous with spray on the stems.

Varnish is useful for dipping or spraying onto seed heads, to give a glossy finish.

Brush on gilt creams—available from art stores—or use a cloth, depending on the effect you need.

TIPS

Care and maintenance of completed arrangements
✿ Never position a finished dried flower display in full sunlight. The materials will dry out and the colors quickly bleach.
✿ Damp is the other enemy to the dried flower arrangement. To prevent any chance of mold developing, keep your displays in a dry place.
✿ Occasionally you may like to clean your arrangement. Use an electric hair dryer (set on cold) and a soft paintbrush. Replace new pieces of material where needed, and spray with clear sealer to give the display a new lease of life.

Recycled containers

A desire to recycle household containers can be a great starting point for creative dried flower arrangements. New ideas can be tried out at no expense, so think before you discard any packaging.

We open food cans of varying shapes and sizes almost every day, along with bottles and jars, and once emptied and thoroughly cleaned, they can be reused, either as they are or covered, for decorative effect. Even shopping bags and empty boxes, once painted with household latex paint, can take on a new lease of life.

When you do come across a food can of a particular shape or size that you could use for a dried flower arrangement, remember to take care when opening the container, in order to leave smooth edges at the mouth of the lid. When considering an arrangement in a recycled container, think about shape and texture. An even, tight group of canes could continue the smooth, industrial look of a round food can, or an organically shaped glass jar may call out for a wild grouping of twisted material or random flower heads.

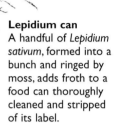

Lepidium can
A handful of *Lepidium sativum*, formed into a bunch and ringed by moss, adds froth to a food can thoroughly cleaned and stripped of its label.

Tall candle pot
This makes a striking display for a candlelit barbecue. For stability in the elements, the cleaned food can has been weighted with stones. A length of hop twine has been wrapped around and glued onto the top and bottom rims of the can. A circle of echinacea surrounds the candle base.

Candle and canes
The rough texture of clipped raspberry canes contrasts with the smooth ivory candle they surround in this cleaned food can. A band of ivory dyed coco moss tied around the tin echoes the candle's look.

Wheat design
Simplicity is the key to this arrangement. A cluster of wheat has been loosely tied together to sit neatly in a fan shape in a rectangular food can. The can is finished with a tied burlap band.

Nutty bag

Paint a brown paper bag with household latex paint, then pad it out with crumpled newspaper and fill with dried materials for a perfect gift. Beechmasts and moss create a stylish feature, finished with a dried orange slice and blue gingham ribbon.

Cinnamon selection

Cover a cleaned rectangular food can with ivory dyed coco moss to give it a different look. The moss is simply tied on with hop twine. This can has been filled with a tightly packed selection of cinnamon sticks.

Green scene

Green dyed coco moss, tied around a food can with green rope, brings out the color of the wheat stalks packed tightly and levelly into the can. The stalks are tied at the top with more green rope.

Fruit bag

Dried oranges nestle in this painted bag which has been partly filled with crumpled newspaper and dry florist's foam, then topped with sphagnum moss and the fruit design. A circle of strung popcorn and blue gingham ribbon add the finishing touches.

Herb chutney
Oregano fills the base of this cleaned chutney jar, and is topped with purple sweet marjoram and a natural hop twine collar.

Spaghetti display
An aesthetically attractive stem of twisted willow has been gilded (see pages 12–15) and set in a spaghetti jar filled with gilded fir cones, to make a stylish corner piece.

Ginger jar
A simple bunch of sage blends with the root ginger that fills the base of this cleaned ginger jar. The garland is a rope twine.

Red stem glass
Striking stems of red *Cornus* have been tied with raffia to sit on a bed of mixed red and white haricot beans in a tall glass.

Memories of a country walk
A collection of dried materials combined in a glass storage jar makes a colorful kitchen display. Use dried herbs, cones, fruit slices, leaves, moss, and bark and aim to make use of varied textures and colors.

Shaker boxes

Round Shaker boxes can be filled with dried
materials to make any number of colorful displays.
Dried red apple slices pile happily into a box bound
with green gingham ribbon. Popcorn adds lightness
to a dark wood box decorated with gingham
and cinnamon. Rich orange slices and peel
can fill a box to the brim, while a pile of
oval boxes painted green, red, and
ivory can be stacked
and decorated with
a string of popcorn
and red gingham to
complement the
filled boxes.

TECHNIQUES AND PROJECTS

Basket and Terracotta Arrangements

The natural hues and textures of baskets and terracotta pots are time-honored accompaniments to dried flowers and plants. Try out the techniques in this section to create romantic set pieces for every corner of the home *(see pages 22–41)*.

Glass, Wire, Urns, Tin, and Wood

Different shapes and textures of container demand different colors and textures of dried flowers. Look at how dramatic effect can be created using voguish containers and the latest in optional extras *(see pages 42–55)*.

Glue Gun Ideas

A glue gun can be used to attach dried plant material to all manner of background and skeletal framework, and in a riot of interesting and enduring colors. Decorate mirrors and photo frames and make flat-backed wall designs using the techniques described in this section *(see pages 56–65)*.

 ## Tied Arrangements

A host of tied dried flower arrangements incorporating different types and sizes of ribbon are covered in this section. These can be used to impart maximum effect to walls and tables (see pages 66–75).

 ## Topiary Trees

Topiary trees are time-consuming but highly rewarding to make. The architectural techniques illustrated in this section bring to life the endless possibilities in terms of shape, color, and texture that make topiary trees so much fun to create (see pages 76–85).

 ## Wired Arrangements

As the dried flower arranger grows in expertise and confidence, he or she can use wiring to make complex creations requiring a greater level of planning and artistry. Look at this section to create beautiful swags, garlands, wreaths, and bunched bowls (see pages 86–101).

 ## Celebrations

Dried flower arrangements are hugely popular at festive occasions and this section will show you how to create displays in glorious color (see pages 102–123).

Tabletop display

This is a simple, modern design that is quick and fun to construct when you can steal a quiet moment to yourself. The materials needed are minimal, and can be adapted to whatever is easily available. To obtain the best effect use materials with single, straight stems and rounded heads. Here we have chosen poppies, roses, and *Nigella*, but *Carthamus*, craspedia, and *Echinops* would work equally well.

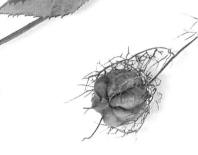

Bright red rose and *Nigella* (green pod)

22

YOU WILL NEED

- **Rectangular rush basket**
- **Dry florist's foam**
- **Knife**
- **Sphagnum moss**
- **22-gauge 12in (30cm) florist's wire**
- **Scissors**
- **Sturdy twigs**
- **Pruning shears**
- **Garden twine**
- ***Nigella* (green pod)**
- **Bright red rose**
- **Poppy (big pod)**
- ***Nigella orientalis***
- **Yellow rose**
- **Lawn moss**

Sphagnum moss

1 Cut dry florist's foam to fit the rush basket tightly and sit 1in (2.5cm) proud of the rim (see pages 12–15).

2 Lightly cover the foam with sphagnum moss and pin in place (see pages 12–15).

3 Cut four twigs of roughly the same height and push them into the foam at each corner of the basket.

4 Cut four more twigs, two long and two short, to connect the corner twigs.

5 Knot a length of garden twine around one of the corner twigs, just above center. Do not cut the twine.

6 Position a horizontal twig by the knot and wrap the twine around it to secure the two twigs together. Knot and cut the twine.

7 Repeat Steps 5–6 to make a fence around the basket.

8 Fill the space inside the fence with mirrored lines of four to five stems of material, all of the same height and quite closely packed together. Start at each short edge by inserting a line of *Nigella* (green pod) stems.

Any straight twig can be used to make the fence and posts: it is easy to make a taller arrangement and have a double or treble layer fence depending on your materials and display area. Aim to be original and don't hesitate to try out your own ideas, colors, and lines. Use different shaped baskets and containers to blend with your home style.

9 In front of the *Nigella* lines insert bright red roses, followed by lines of medium-sized poppies.

10 Next insert rows of *Nigella orientalis*, followed by a single row of yellow roses in the center.

11 Pin some lawn moss all around the stems and to the rim of the basket to accentuate the green rushes.

12 To finish, insert individual heads of *Nigella orientalis* all around the rim of the basket, quite closely packed together.

Traditional basket

A romantic and timeless arrangement, this English basket display makes a wonderful gift, or table or fireplace decoration.

Peonies and roses are enchanting, arranged on their own or mixed with country flowers, as demonstrated here with larkspur and *Gomphrena globosa*. Both peonies and roses benefit from being steamed open prior to use for a special finish. Hold the flower head over a steaming kettle to allow the petals to soften, then tweak the petals into shape, being careful not to scald yourself.

Dark pink larkspur and *Setaria glauca*

YOU WILL NEED

- **Traditional basket**
- **Newspaper**
- **Dry florist's foam**
- **Knife**
- **Sphagnum moss**
- **Binding wire**
- **Scissors**
- **22-gauge 12in (30cm) florist's wire**
- **Light pink larkspur**
- **Echinacea**
- **Red amaranthus**
- ***Setaria glauca***
- **Dark pink larkspur**
- **Dark pink *Celosia***
- **Purple *Helichrysum***
- ***Setaria italica***
- **Pink peony**
- **Pink *Gomphrena globosa***
- **Dark red roses**
- **Wide, pink voile ribbon**

Echinacea and dark pink *Celosia*

1 Part fill the basket with crumpled newspaper. Cut a dry florist's foam square to sit in the center of the basket about ½–1in (1.5–2.5cm) proud of the rim. Position the foam on top of the newspaper and pack in around the sides with sphagnum moss.

2 Thread binding wire through the weaving, over the foam, through the weaving on the other side, and back over the foam. Twist the wire in the weaving and cut. Repeat to make a cross of wire over the foam.

3 Pin sphagnum moss all over the foam (see pages 12–15).

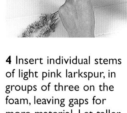

4 Insert individual stems of light pink larkspur, in groups of three on the foam, leaving gaps for more material. Let taller stems in the center fan out to shorter stems around the sides.

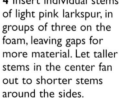

5 Build up the display by adding individual stems of material, again evenly distributed and fanning out all over. Start with echinacea.

6 Add red amaranthus and *Setaria glauca* individually or in groups of two or three. Let the grass stems stand proud of the other material.

7 Add dark pink larkspur.

8 Break off the large pink *Celosia* heads and individually wire them (see pages 12–15). Insert these all over.

The speed of flower arranging comes with practice so allow plenty of time to complete the display, and a few minutes to tweak the final design.

Enjoy collecting small amounts of your favorite garden flowers for this luxurious display, saving the perfect peony or rose for the finishing touch.

9 Wire up bunches of five to seven stems of purple *Helichrysum* and add to the arrangement. Stand back from your work frequently to check the overall balance of color and material.

10 Insert *Setaria italica* stems and pink peonies, and wired bunches of six to eight stems of pink *Gomphrena*.

11 Finally, fill the gaps with dark red roses.

12 Fold a length of ribbon into a double bow with one tail longer than the other. Use 22-gauge wire to secure it in the middle (see pages 12–15). Push the wire of the bow into the foam, close to the rim of the basket.

Corner display

Dark corners can quickly be enlivened with this colorful display incorporating a nut stick basket and raspberry canes, completed with a front cane bunch. Alternatively, you could choose a copper box or complementary colored container for a less rustic look. First study the proportions of the corner, then select a suitable display table or pedestal of the required height on which to display your arrangement. Try the container in the space,

Tansy and bearded wheat

BASKET AND TERRACOTTA ARRANGEMENTS

YOU WILL NEED

- **Dry florist's foam**
- **Square nut sticks basket**
- **Knife**
- **Sphagnum moss**
- **22-gauge 12in (30cm) florist's wire**
- **Scissors**
- **Raspberry canes**
- **Dark blue larkspur**
- **Bearded wheat**
- **Tansy**
- *Centaurea macrocephala*
- **Red broom bloom**
- **Palm**
- **Wheat**
- *Nigella orientalis*
- **Yellow rose**
- **Red *Helichrysum***
- **Green garden twine**

1 Cut a square of dry florist's foam to fit the base of the basket and stand about 2in (5cm) proud of the rim. Place a little sphagnum moss on the floor of the basket and position the foam on top. Pack in around the sides of the foam with more moss.

2 Pin moss all over the foam (see pages 12–15).

Centaurea macrocephala

3 This corner arrangement uses layers of materials to form a triangle, with the

tallest materials at the back. Cut about five tall, three medium, and three short raspberry canes. Push the canes, one at a time, into the foam slightly right of center and toward the arrangement's back with the tallest at the back, the medium height canes in the middle, and the shortest canes in front.

4 Cut about seven or eight stems of dark blue larkspur slightly shorter than the tallest raspberry canes and push these into the foam to the right of the canes at the back. Cut seven to eight stems of bearded wheat to roughly the same height and insert these to the left of the canes, also toward the back.

5 Cut about four stems of tansy and six of *Centaurea macrocephala* to differing heights, but shorter than the larkspur and wheat, and arrange these staggering from back to front through the arrangement's center.

6 Push about five stems of red broom bloom into the foam in front of the larkspur and let some palm fan out to the right.

checking that the container's depth does not dominate the piece: you want more flowers than container when the design is complete. Remember, too, that corner arrangements are seen from the sides as well as the front, so it is a good idea to check the design in the corner frequently throughout the construction process.

This modern arrangement uses dramatic primary colors, but you can, of course, adapt the materials to suit your taste.

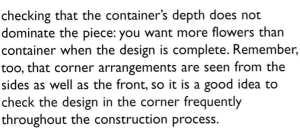

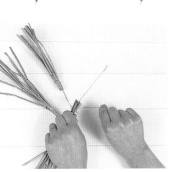

center, yellow rose right of center, more palm at the sides, and *Centaurea* blooms to fill any gaps at the very front. Add wired-up bunches of red *Helichrysum* to the left of the yellow roses. Push the wheat stalk bunches into the foam at the side extremes.

7 Wire four bunches of wheat, of about eight to ten stalks each, and shorter than the palm using 22-gauge wire (see pages 12–15).

The stiff sticks and raspberry canes impart a strong central line to the final display. This contrasts with the colorful movement created by the large yellow thistle heads.

8 Start to fill out the design, working from the back to the front, by inserting individual stems, cut to different heights, of wheat, through the middle, *Nigella orientalis* and more larkspur left of

9 Wire up a small bunch each of wheat, bearded wheat, and raspberry canes—about three to five stems per bunch, keeping the wire ends at right angles to the bunches (see pages

12–15). Tie green garden twine over the wire. Insert these bunches at the front of the display so that they lie almost horizontally across the top of the basket.

TIP

❀ Cut wheat stalks on an angle to create a sharp point that will make them easier to insert into the foam.

Wall bouquet

Wall bouquets can be created in all sizes to suit any area to be decorated. Therefore you can adapt the basic principles of this project to accommodate larger, smaller, or thinner spaces. Once you have viewed the surroundings and proportions of the wall area, collect together the materials. Gather a range of pointed, spiky, and round flowers and seed heads; the top of the bouquet needs points while round flower heads suit the center of the display. It is usually better to create quite an organized arrangement: this technique does not favor a disorderly look.

'Hen and Chickens' poppies, sprayed basil green

YOU WILL NEED

- **Dry florist's foam**
- **Knife**
- **12in (30cm) flat, round cane base**
- **Binding wire**
- **Scissors**
- **Sphagnum moss**
- **22-gauge 12in (30cm) florist's wire**
- **Stem binding tape**
- *Solidago*
- *Nigella orientalis*
- **Red broom bloom**
- **'Hen and Chickens' poppy, sprayed basil green**
- **Red *Protea repens***
- **Orange tagetes**
- **Dark red zinnia**
- **Yellow zinnia**
- **Red dyed oak leaves**
- **Yellow achillea**
- **Orange *Gomphrena globosa***
- **Glue gun**
- **Wide, lime green satin ribbon**

Red *Protea repens*

1 Cut a block of dry florist's foam to 7 x 6in (18 x 15cm). Wire the foam in the center of a flat cane base. Thread binding wire through the weaving, over the foam, through the weaving on the other side, and back over the foam. Secure the wire in the weaving and cut.

2 Pin sphagnum moss all over the foam (see pages 12–15).

3 Wrap 22-gauge florist's wires with stem binding tape, and bend in half to form a hanger. Thread the wire through the base at the intended top of the bouquet, opposite one shorter edge of the foam block. Twist the wire ends together to make a loop (see pages 12–15).

4 Insert individual stems of material into the foam to build up the arrangement, which has a round, domed shape. Use *Solidago* in small groups of three to four stems, about 5–6in (13–15cm) long. Position the tallest group centrally at the top of the bouquet to guide the height of the whole piece. Insert another, shorter group on the right to start the side shape. Push in two shorter groups at the bottom corners.

5 Add a tall group of *Nigella orientalis* to the right of the tallest *Solidago*, and a shorter group bottom right, by the corner *Solidago*.

6 Position tall groups of red broom bloom, close to the cane base, top right, under the *Solidago*, and top left. Insert a smaller group bottom right, under the *Nigella*. Insert poppies, in groups of two or three, in the center top, and the top left, next to the left broom bloom. Stagger two red *Protea* top center, next to the poppies. Place the arrangement against a wall to check it has an even shape. Remember to fill in material close to the base and up the sides of the foam.

Any flat, strong, rush, cane, or basket base can be purchased ready-made. Always choose one smaller than the final, desired size of the bouquet, and note that you must be able to thread wire through it to secure foam in place.

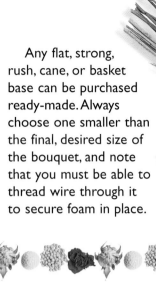

7 Insert groups of three to four heads of orange tagetes, dark red zinnia, and yellow zinnia staggered through the center, keeping an eye on color balance.

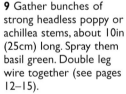

The profusion of flowers in this dramatic display will warm up the dullest of rooms, but the bouquet is an ideal complement to the color of Mediterranean and Aztec fabrics.

9 Gather bunches of strong headless poppy or achillea stems, about 10in (25cm) long. Spray them basil green. Double leg wire together (see pages 12–15).

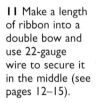

11 Make a length of ribbon into a double bow and use 22-gauge wire to secure it in the middle (see pages 12–15).

12 Push the wire of the bow into the foam just above the stalk bunches.

8 Use red oak leaves and yellow achillea to fill in, checking the bouquet is evenly rounded. Use orange *Gomphrena* to add color where needed.

10 Insert the wired stem bunches at the center bottom, glue, and trim.

Fireplace feature

Zea mays corn husks, chili peppers, and blood orange slices

Fireplaces often benefit from a dried flower arrangement to soften and draw attention away from the empty grate during the summer months, or simply to add interest to the area when the fire is not lit.

This stunning feature with a wheat background is easy to design in different colorways by changing the front border, while retaining the design's chunkiness. To make an impact you will need enough wheat to make a thick background.

Proportions are important with a fireplace display, as it will be viewed from all conceivable positions, so remember to check the arrangement from all sides.

YOU WILL NEED

- **Nut sticks trough**
- **Dry florist's foam**
- **Knife**
- **Sphagnum moss**
- **Binding wire**
- **Scissors**
- **22-gauge 12in (30cm) florist's wire**
- **Wheat**
- **7 carline thistles**
- **2 bell cups**
- **Poppy (big pod)**
- *Nigella orientalis*
- **Terracotta dyed** *Carthamus*
- **8 artichoke heads**
- *Protea compacta*
- **Red** *Helichrysum*
- *Zea mays* **corn husks**
- **Blood orange slices**
- **Apple slices**
- **Chili peppers**

1 Cut dry florist's foam to fit the trough and stand about 2in (5cm) proud of the rim (see pages 12–15). Place a little sphagnum moss on the floor of the basket and position the foam on top. Pack in around the sides of the foam with moss.

2 Wrap binding wire around a top nut stick, pass it over the foam, around the stick on the other side, and back over the foam. Twist the wire around the stick and cut. Repeat at a second interval along the trough.

3 Pin sphagnum moss all over the foam (see pages 12–15).

4 Individually insert stems of wheat, in staggered pairs at the back of the trough, so that the tallest stems in the center fan out to shorter stems at the sides.

5 Add in another three to five shorter rows of fanned wheat, ensuring there are no large gaps.

6 Carefully cut off the leaves of seven carline thistle, leaving a few at the top for decoration. Insert two thistles staggered centrally in front of the wheat.

7 Add two bell cups in front of the thistles, close to the trough edge.

8 Start to build up the low arrangement at the front. Insert three thistles at the right edge and two on the far left. Insert individual stems of poppy in groups of ten, one on the right and one, slightly higher, left of center.

Clean up your workspace regularly, keeping extra wheat stalks to make bundles, because it is easier to see clearly when working over an empty surface.

For an alternative color scheme, this resplendent fan of wheat could be replaced by twigs, peacock feathers, or pink or blue larkspur, and the accompanying plants by pink Helichrysum, peonies, and roses.

9 Wire two thick bunches of *Nigella* stems, wrapping the wire around the middle and keeping the wire ends at right angles to the bunches (see pages 12–15). Insert the bunches at the very front, to the left of each poppy group, one pointing down, the other up.

10 Insert stems of terracotta *Carthamus* to spill over the left edge and fill the gap between the poppies and *Nigella* on the right.

11 Pull out the purple tops of eight artichoke heads. Individually insert three heads on the left of the bell cups and five at the far right.

12 Insert four to five *Protea compacta* between the poppies and *Nigella* on the left and above the poppies on the far right.

13 Wire four bunches of red *Helichrysum* (see pages 12–15) and evenly spread them out around the display. Stand back from your work regularly to judge overall balance.

14 Double leg wire together (see pages 12–15) a few corn husks and insert center front, bottom right, and top left.

15 Wire together two groups of four to five blood orange slices (see pages 12–15) and stagger them to the left of the display.

16 Wire a bunch of four to five apple slices and insert above the *Nigella*, right of center.

17 Wire up three bunches of chili peppers. Insert the chilies center front, spilling over the edge of the trough. Wash your hands after handling chilies.

Carline thistle

Tiny terracotta pots

Great fun can be derived from making dried arrangements in tiny terracotta pots. You could make individual candle pots as gifts, or to decorate the table at a special dinner party. Try placing a selection of small candle pots on a mirror as a table center, or create table favors for a wedding. Tiny filled pots also make excellent and inexpensive thank-you gifts.

These tiny pots can easily be covered by gluing on very small amounts of materials such

Red rose

YOU WILL NEED

- **2in (5cm) terracotta pots**
- **Scissors**
- **Glue gun**

For the Rope pot
- **Green rope**

For the Chinese lantern pot
- **Chinese lanterns**

For the Candle pot
- **Dry florist's foam**
- **Knife**
- **Sphagnum moss**
- **22-gauge 12in (30cm) florist's wire**
- **White candle, 1in (2.5cm) diameter and 4in (10cm) high**
- **2 small strictum cones, or 1 large one cut in half**
- **Tiny alder cones**
- **Tiny amounts of fungi and chili pepper**
- **A few red beans**
- **Dried lemon slice**
- **Green reindeer moss**
- **Raffia**

Rope pot

1 Take a length of green rope long enough to wrap all around the outside of a 2in (5cm) terracotta pot. Starting at the bottom of the pot, use a glue gun to apply a little glue at a time and wind the rope around the pot over the glue. Keep the rope wraps close together.

2 When you reach the top of the pot, glue the end of the rope very firmly in place to neatly finish the decoration.

Chinese lantern pot

1 Take a small selection of Chinese lanterns of different sizes. Pull open each head and cut it into sections. Use your hand to slightly flatten each section.

2 Start at the top of a 2in (5cm) pot, using the largest Chinese lantern pieces. Apply a little glue to the pot rim and stick down the first Chinese lantern section so that it is a little proud of the top of the pot. Glue down

subsequent pieces that slightly overlap all around the rim, pressing down well as you go.

3 Cover the pot with a second and third row of Chinese lantern sections, making sure each row just overlaps the bottom of the previous one. At the bottom of the pot fold the edges of the Chinese lantern pieces to meet the base of the pot, and glue very firmly.

as pieces of fabric, burlap, or rope for a textured look and feel. You can also try dried leaves, rose or hydrangea petals, cinnamon sticks, raspberry canes, or moss. Take a little time to consider your options and think up your own designs and styles.

Red rose petals, individually glued on, disguise the terracotta pot beneath.

A single red rose with a gold leaf stands in a gilded pot (see pages 12–15).

Candle pot

1 Cut dry florist's foam to fit a 2in (5cm) terracotta pot level with the top and fix it in place (see pages 12–15). Cover the foam lightly with sphagnum moss and pin in place with 22-gauge florist's wire (see pages 12–15).

2 Wire up the candle with 22-gauge florist's wire (see pages 12–15) and position it in the pot's center.

4 Build up the design by gluing in very small amounts of fungi, chili pepper, and red beans on their ends. Keep the arrangement at the candle base so that the material does not burn when the candle is lit.

Bay leaves make great cover material.

3 Start by gluing two strictum cones and a few tiny alder cones in attractive positions around the candle.

5 Cut a dried lemon slice in half and glue the pieces on each side of the candle. Fill in any gaps by gluing in some green reindeer moss and finish with a tiny raffia bow.

Garden bowl

Terracotta bowls are wonderfully versatile, and here a bowl is used to house a selection of dried flowers, miniature garden tools, and small terracotta pots to create an original design for a summer barbecue picnic bench or the kitchen supper table. Arrangements like this often evolve as they go along, so don't hesitate to experiment with new ideas.

It is a good idea to collect together interesting material as and when you see it, such as twigs, cones, perhaps leftover large seeds and packets, various stalks, and garden labels.

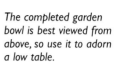

The completed garden bowl is best viewed from above, so use it to adorn a low table.

YOU WILL NEED

- **Dry florist's foam**
- **Knife**
- **Terracotta bowl, 10in (25cm) diameter and 4in (10cm) high**
- **Sphagnum moss**
- **22-gauge 12in (30cm) florist's wire**
- **Scissors**
- **Lavender**
- **Cream *Santolina***
- **8 strictum cones**
- **3 miniature garden tools**
- **Miniature bucket**
- **Glue gun**
- **4 1in (2.5cm) terracotta pots**
- **2in (5cm) terracotta pot**
- **2 terracotta labels**
- **Orange tagetes**
- **Extra *Santolina* stalks**
- **Green or natural garden twine**
- **Green reindeer moss**

1 Cut some dry florist's foam to pack the terracotta bowl tightly and sit proud of the rim by 2in (5cm). Pin sphagnum moss in place over the foam with 22-gauge florist's wire (see pages 12–15).

2 Make three bunches of lavender about 7in (18cm) long, each with about 40 staggered heads. Wire the bunches halfway along, leaving the ends of the wire at a right angle to the bunch (see pages 12–15). Use the same wiring technique to make five bunches of cream *Santolina* about 4in (10cm) long and of a similar thickness to the lavender bunches. Keep the *Santolina* stalks that you cut off for use later.

3 Imagine the bowl divided into three sections. Push a lavender bunch into each third so that the heads protrude over the bowl's edge, inserting the wire ends into the foam.

4 Wire up the strictum cones, miniature tools, and miniature bucket (see pages 12–15). The small terracotta pots used here do not have holes at their base so are glued in place, but pots with holes can be wired. The terracotta labels do not need any preparation since they will simply be pushed into the foam.

5 Begin to add the materials to the arrangement, still working in the three sections of the lavender. In the first section, position three 1in (2.5cm) pots together with three cones and a miniature spade. Fix an upturned bucket with two cones falling out of it in the second section, along with a miniature hoe and fork. In the final section, position the remaining 1in (2.5cm) pot and a 2in (5cm) pot, two labels spaced out on the rim, and the remaining three cones.

6 Add in the *Santolina* bunches, two staggered just above and next to the labels and the remainder in a similar arrangement close to the spade.

7 Individually wire nine to twelve orange tagetes (see pages 12–15) if the stalks are not strong enough to be inserted directly into the foam. Arrange the tagetes so that three or four flowers sit in each third of the bowl.

8 Gather the *Santolina* stalks kept from Step 2, and some extra, and form them into seven bunches of about 40 stems, roughly 3in (7.5cm) long. Wire the stalk bunches toward the center and cover the wire with garden twine. Intersperse the bunches into the bowl. Fill in any gaps with green reindeer moss.

Tiny tools

Candle trough

The materials used to surround the candle have been specifically chosen to complement the decoration on the trough.

Candles and terracotta are natural companions, the warmth of the terracotta color blending subtly with the ivory of beeswax church candles. This painted Aztec trough with hues of copper and blue brings out the richness of the oranges in the arrangement while contrasting well with the strong deep blue lavender. Bunches of wheat and lavender zigzag haphazardly echoing the Aztec design of the base. Look for a commercially painted container like this, or design your own by applying household latex or artists' acrylic paints.

YOU WILL NEED

- **Newspaper**
- **Wheat**
- **Copper spray paint**
- **Trough, 9 x 6 x 6in (23 x 15 x 15cm)**
- **Dry florist's foam**
- **Knife**
- **Sphagnum moss**
- **22-gauge 12in (30cm) florist's wire**
- **Scissors**
- **White candle, 2in (5cm) diameter and 12in (30cm) high**
- **White candle, 2in (5cm) diameter and 8in (20cm) high**
- **Barbecue skewers or cocktail sticks**
- **Anchor tape**
- **Lavender**
- **Glue gun**
- **3 2in (5cm) terracotta pots**
- **1.5in (3cm) terracotta pot**
- **1in (2.5cm) terracotta pot**
- **5 lantern oranges**
- **Orange slices**
- **Beechmasts**

1 Cover your work surface with newspaper and spray about 27 ears of wheat with copper paint, following the paint manufacturer's instructions.

2 Half fill a trough with crumpled newspaper. Cut some dry florist's foam to pack the trough and sit proud of the rim by 2in (5cm) (see pages 12–15). Cover the foam lightly with sphagnum moss and pin in place with 22-gauge florist's wire (see pages 12–15).

3 Mount the two candles on skewers with anchor tape and fix them firmly in the center of the trough.

4 Make eight chunky bunches of lavender, about 5–6in (13–15cm) long with roughly 40 stems per bunch. Using a full 12in (30cm) 22-gauge wire, bind tightly around the center of the bunch, keeping the wire ends at a right angle to the bunch (see pages 12–15). Similarly, make nine shorter bunches of copper wheat using three large heads, or more if smaller.

5 Push the wire ends of the lavender bunches into the dry foam, so that the heads point out over the trough's edge. You will need to cross over the stalks. In the same way, insert the wheat bunches in the spaces left by the lavender.

6 Use a glue gun to fix the terracotta pots in place. Position a 2in (5cm) pot centrally in front of the two candles, with the two smaller pots on top. On the other side centrally position the remaining 2in (5cm) pots.

7 Wire up five whole lantern oranges (see pages 12–15). Push them into place, two on one side and to the right of the taller candle, and three on the opposite corner by the shorter candle. Gather groups of two to three orange slices and glue these in throughout the trough to balance the arrangement.

8 Glue beechmasts over any still-visible wire and fill in any gaps by pushing in, gluing, or wiring in more moss.

Sprayed copper wheat and orange slices

Kitchen pot

Terracotta is a natural companion to any plant material, but terracotta pots can also be painted, sponged, or gilded to complement the style of your kitchen. You could try out a verdigris kit or other paint effects, or use varied stencil designs in any color combination. You may want to paint a pot to blend in with the color of your ceramics and textiles, or leave it natural to fit in with baskets and wood tones.

This pot has been lightly gilded just around the rim.

Cream
Carthamus

YOU WILL NEED

- **Gold gilt cream**
- **8in (20cm) terracotta pot**
- **Newspaper**
- **Dry florist's foam**
- **Knife**
- **Sphagnum moss**
- **22-gauge 12in (30cm) florist's wire**
- **Scissors**
- *Lepidium sativum*
- **Wheat**
- **2 4in (10cm) terracotta pots**
- **18-gauge 12in (30cm) florist's wire**
- **Bay (fresh or dry)**
- **White larkspur**
- *Sorghum nigrum*
- **'Hen and Chickens' poppy**
- **Cream *Carthamus***
- **Thyme**
- **Sage**
- **4 *Zea mays* strawberry corncobs**
- **Glue gun**

1 Use some gold gilt cream to lightly gild the rim of an 8in (20cm) terracotta pot (pages 12–15).

2 Fill the base of the pot with crumpled newspaper. Cut some dry florist's foam to pack the pot tightly, allowing 2in (5cm) to remain proud at the rim (see pages 12–15). Lightly cover the foam with sphagnum moss and pin in place using 22-gauge florist's wire (see pages 12–15).

3 Starting with the *Lepidium sativum*, cut a group of individual stems about two and a half times the height of the pot and insert them into the foam at the back. Cut a second bunch of *Lepidium* slightly shorter than the first, and individually push the stems into the foam to the right of the previous bunch. Cut a third bunch of *Lepidium* about half the height of the first, and push these into place to the left of the first group.

4 Cut one tall, one medium, and two short bunches of wheat. Push the tall wheat stalks into the foam in front of the *Lepidium* at the back. Insert the medium-height stalks to the right of the *Lepidium* on the right. Push the two smallest bunches in at left of center and to the front left of the arrangement.

5 Wire up two 4in (10cm) terracotta pots, using 18-gauge wire for these reasonably heavy pots (see pages 12–15). Position the pots centrally, one below the other, slightly staggered.

6 Insert individual stalks of bay into the foam at varying angles. Stand back at regular intervals to check the arrangement's overall shape.

Zea mays **strawberry corncob**

Here, the kitchen pot arrangement is kept natural in design, to bring interest and tranquillity to a busy room. A terracotta pot is perfectly at home filled with wheats, poppies, corns, and any selection of herbs you can find. Wheat retains its color well, so is ideal in a light kitchen setting. Plan your harvesting in advance to give yourself a wide collection, and let your creative tendencies make the center of the home a truly vibrant place.

This tall arrangement is best displayed at eye level, for full impact.

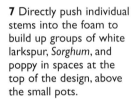

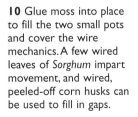

7 Directly push individual stems into the foam to build up groups of white larkspur, *Sorghum*, and poppy in spaces at the top of the design, above the small pots.

8 Insert short stems of cream *Carthamus*, thyme, and sage in groups to build up the lower sides and front of the design.

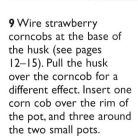

9 Wire strawberry corncobs at the base of the husk (see pages 12–15). Pull the husk over the corncob for a different effect. Insert one corn cob over the rim of the pot, and three around the two small pots.

10 Glue moss into place to fill the two small pots and cover the wire mechanics. A few wired leaves of *Sorghum* impart movement, and wired, peeled-off corn husks can be used to fill in gaps.

TIPS
✿ The herbs used in this arrangement can be varied as available.
✿ Cut wheat stalks at an angle to create sharp points that will make them easier to insert into the foam.
✿ You could also fill a pot in the same way using other materials that match your kitchen's color scheme, such as colored moss, rope, fruits, herbs, and raffia.

Garden display

Think of how a garden flower border blends different textures and shapes, the plants intertwining to form a palette of varying heights. This is the effect you should attempt to recreate in this dried flower arrangement.

We have used strong, vivid colors to accompany fashionable Aztec fabrics with their red, orange, green, and yellow colorways. Textures in this display are all-important: proteas, mushrooms, and cones create a strong, rough appearance.

Sponge mushroom

YOU WILL NEED

- **Basket trough**
- **Newspaper**
- **Dry florist's foam**
- **Knife**
- **Sphagnum moss**
- **22-gauge 12in (30cm) florist's wire**
- **Scissors**
- **Eucalyptus, sprayed basil green**
- *Sorghum nigrum*
- **Red *Protea repens***
- **Green amaranthus**
- **Cream *Carthamus*, sprayed basil green**
- Yellow *Santolina*
- **Red dyed achillea**
- **18-gauge 12in (30cm) florist's wire**
- **Glue gun**
- **Sponge mushroom**
- **Craspedia**
- **9 red roses**
- **6 pine cones**
- **10 artificial apples**
- **Red zinnia**

1 Half fill the trough with crumpled newspaper then pack in dry florist's foam so that it sits about 1in (2.5cm) proud of the rim. Pin sphagnum moss all over the foam (see pages 12–15).

2 This rectangular display is, to begin with, formed with a definite back, middle, and front. Start by inserting about six stems of green sprayed eucalyptus roughly evenly spaced apart all along the back. Remember that the plants at the rear of the display must be the tallest.

3 Push five to seven stems of *Sorghum*, of slightly differing heights, into the foam next to and in front of each eucalyptus stem.

4 In the gaps between the eucalyptus and *Sorghum*, insert three staggered pairs of red *Protea*.

5 Start to fill in the basket, with the taller material at the back. Push in pairs of green amaranthus in the back row gaps. Insert single stems of cream *Carthamus* in pairs, threes, or fours directly in front of the back row. Wire up about four medium length and three short bunches of yellow *Santolina*—two to three stems per bunch— using 22-gauge wire (see pages 12–15). Insert the short bunches at the front and the longer ones in between and behind. Insert three pairs of red dyed achillea, one bloom staggered in front of the other, evenly spaced across the middle toward the front of the display.

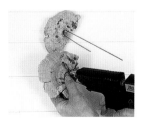

6 Glue a bent 18-gauge wire to a piece of sponge mushroom (see pages 12–15). Wire up three more mushrooms.

While working, remember to refer back to thoughts of the garden border and don't be too regimented; most plants don't stand to attention but mingle together. Choose a chunky container that complements the flowers used. Try it in the position you are designing for, and look at the design in position as you build it up, adding extra interest where needed.

Red dyed achillea and red zinnia

9 Individually insert roses in groups of three next to the craspedia.

10 Wire up six pine cones and nine artificial apples (see pages 12–15). Push the cones into the foam in the gaps in the middle of the arrangement and the apples toward the front. Stand back from your work frequently to judge its balance.

11 Wire up bunches of about three stalks of red zinnia and use them to fill in gaps in the middle and front sections of the trough. Use a selection of material of your choice to fill any remaining gaps.

8 Insert 12 craspedia stems to form four groups of three, slightly staggered in height, in the gaps along the back.

7 Push the mushrooms into the foam at the front of the arrangement, some positioned horizontally, others at a slight angle.

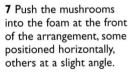

Display your garden on a pine dresser, against a buttermilk background, or as a colorful feature for the fireplace during the summer months.

Terracotta pot wall hanging

To give yourself a treat, find a day to yourself, or share it with a friend, and enjoy making this wall hanging.

Wall hangings are an ideal way to add color and interest to walls, beams, arches, and to brighten a dark area on the stairway or hall. This large design uses a variety of textures, and mixes colors to achieve a dramatic finish. Choose your materials carefully, aiming to incorporate different shapes, and never underestimate the power of green to bring out the vibrancy of other colors.

YOU WILL NEED

- **Chicken wire, 16in (40cm) wide and 26in (66cm) long**
- **Wire cutters**
- **Sphagnum moss**
- **Block of dry florist's foam**
- **Knife**
- **Binding wire**
- **Scissors**
- **18-gauge 12in (30cm) florist's wire**
- **Green stem binding tape**
- **22-gauge 12in (30cm) florist's wire**
- **Red dyed and treated oak leaf**
- *Solidago*
- **'Hen and Chickens' poppy, sprayed basil green**

- **Golden zinnia**
- **Burgundy zinnia**
- *Nigella orientalis*
- **Red *Gomphrena globosa***
- **Yellow achillea**
- **Red broom bloom**
- **8 red *Protea repens***
- **5 *Protea compacta***
- **3 4in (10cm) terracotta pots**
- **3 3in (7.5cm) terracotta pots**
- **20 vine sticks**
- **Red raffia**
- **3 large fir cones**
- **Glue gun**
- **Yellow dyed coco moss**

Red *Protea repens*

1 Lay a length of chicken wire flat and place a layer of moss down the center of the wire. Cut a block of florist's foam in half lengthwise. Position the two foam blocks on the moss and add more moss to the sides and on top of the blocks.

2 Wrap the chicken wire around the foam and moss to form a parcel. Twist the wire ends together neatly and push the ends back into the moss to avoid scratching. Wrap the complete parcel with binding wire for added strength.

3 Bend an 18-gauge wire wrapped with stem binding tape in half to make a hanger (see pages 12–15). Fix the hanger in place at the top of the parcel, onto an area of chicken wire that does not form the join (see pages 12–15).

4 Use 22-gauge wire to make small bunches of two or three stalks of poppy, red oak leaf, *Solidago*, golden zinnia, burgundy zinnia, *Nigella orientalis*, red *Gomphrena*, yellow achillea, and red broom bloom, keeping the wire ends at right angles to the bunches (see pages 12–15). Individually wire six red *Protea repens* and four *Protea compacta*.

5 Make two bunches of about 10 vine sticks, 8–9in (20–23cm) long. Cover the wire that binds them with red raffia. Wire up three large fir cones (see pages 12–15).

6 Start to insert your materials into the foam block and moss parcel, working with one plant variety at a time to help you visualize the overall balance as you work. Begin by pushing in the wire ends of the oak leaf, *Solidago*, and poppy.

7 Wire up six terracotta pots (see pages 12–15). Space them in a staggered line down the center of the wall hanging, wire them up in place, and secure these relatively heavy pots by pushing any sturdy stem through the hole in the base to wedge it in. Add the vine sticks tied up with red raffia on either side of the pots.

8 Add the wired cones, one top right, one center left, and one centrally toward the bottom. Hold the hanging up to the wall at regular intervals to check that you are filling out the sides as well as the front.

9 Insert the six wired red *Protea repens* staggered around the center of the design from top to bottom. Add *Protea compacta* in two pairs centrally. Now add bunches of golden and burgundy zinnia and *Nigella orientalis*.

10 Use red *Gomphrena*, yellow achillea, and red broom bloom to fill in any gaps still left in the wall hanging. Check the edges again. Fill the flower pots by gluing in the last *Protea*
compacta, a few poppies, red *Protea repens*, and yellow dyed coco moss. Push more coco moss into the foam to fill any other small gaps.

The rich warmth of the colors of the wall hanging can look even more stunning against a pine backdrop.

Classical urn

An inexpensive urn like this can be found in junk shops or garage sales, and the most uninteresting urns can be transformed with a little paint or gilt cream.

This fan design looks great in pairs, at either end of a mantelpiece, or in front of a mirror: remember to fill in the back if it is to be reflected in the mirror. If you can't find two matching urns, why not use two different sizes to create an interesting display.

The gold of the candle links to that of the urn, creating the perfect memento for a golden wedding anniversary.

YOU WILL NEED

- **Newspaper**
- **Small urn**
- **Gold florist's spray paint**
- **Dry florist's foam**
- **Knife**
- **Sphagnum moss**
- **22-gauge 12in (30cm) florist's wire**
- **Scissors**
- **Peach dyed wheat**
- **Poppy (big pod)**
- **White larkspur**
- *Nigella orientalis*
- **5 peach roses**
- **Terracotta achillea**

1 Cover your work surface with newspaper and spray a small urn with gold paint, following the manufacturer's instructions.

2 Slice a square of dry florist's foam at an angle at the corners so that it can wedge into the narrow base of the urn. The foam needs to sit proud of the rim by about 1in (2.5cm). Pin in sphagnum moss to cover the foam (see pages 12–15).

3 This arrangement forms a fan shape starting with the tallest material in the center and working forward by layering shorter materials. Each new flower material should be only a little shorter than the one before, and the extent of gradation between materials should be roughly equal. Take about 25 tall stems of peach dyed wheat and cut and push them into the foam so that the tallest stems fan out to shorter stems at the sides.

4 Cut about 14 poppy stems so that, when pushed into the foam, the pods are no lower than the ears of wheat. Insert the poppies in front of the wheat, forming a fan shape as before. Use the poppies with the thickest pods at the sides, and the thin pods in the center to accentuate the height in the arrangement's center.

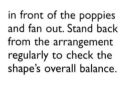

in front of the poppies and fan out. Stand back from the arrangement regularly to check the shape's overall balance.

5 Cut white larkspur stems so that the flowers sit just below the poppy pods when inserted. Push the stems into the foam

6 Push a fanned out row of *Nigella orientalis* into the foam in front of the larkspur.

Poppy (big pod)

Variety of texture, as always, is an important aspect of adding interest, and in this case you also need to pay attention to detail to ensure a uniform shape. The peach wheat and roses blend beautifully with the crackled antique gold of the urn, the white of the larkspur bringing the design to life.

9 Fill in the back of the arrangement from the base of the wheat ears to the rim of the urn with white larkspur fans.

A warm, stylized look to enhance the elegance of a hallway or formal setting. The soft, peach roses carry the color through from the more orderly wheat fan.

7 Cut off the heads of five peach roses, leaving some stem to insert into the foam: the roses need to sit just a little lower than the *Nigella orientalis*. Insert one rose centrally and fan out two on either side.

10 Insert a few very short stems of *Nigella orientalis* around the rim of the urn to cover the moss and finish the display.

TIP

❀ Cut wheat stalks at an angle to create a sharp point that will make them easier to insert into the foam.

8 To finish the front, fill the triangular gap with terracotta achillea.

A small urn has been transformed by a glorious pyramid of color.

Glass vase

How many of us have a glass spaghetti jar lingering unused at the back of a kitchen cabinet? Well dig it out, blow away the cobwebs, and turn it into the basis for a contemporary dried flower arrangement. This display is particularly suited to a modern setting of glass, iron, steel, white walls, and contemporary art, or positioned alone with a low glass bowl of fruits, or near a stylish recycled glass platter.

Allium stems and head

YOU WILL NEED

- **Tall glass sphagetti jar**
- *Allium* **heads and stem, sprayed basil green**
- **Scissors**
- **Dry florist's foam sphere**
- **Knife**
- **Glue gun**
- **Sphagnum moss**
- **22-gauge 12in (30cm) florist's wire**
- **Green lantern oranges or lantern limes**
- **Artichoke heads**
- **Basil green florist's spray paint (optional)**
- **Dark pink rose**
- **Apple slices**
- **Light green reindeer moss**
- **Gold-coated wire**

1 Cut *Allium* heads away from the stalks, leaving some stem on the head to push into the foam later; you will use more stalks than heads. Cut the stalks so they are ½–1in (1.5–2.5cm) taller than the vase.

2 Fill the vase with *Allium* stalks, for aesthetic reasons arranging the stalks on a slight diagonal. Trim the stems so they are all level, about ½in (1.5cm) above the rim of the vase.

3 Cut a dry florist's foam sphere in half.

4 Push the half sphere firmly and centrally onto the *Allium* stems and secure with glue.

5 Lightly cover the foam with sphagnum moss and pin in place (see pages 12–15).

6 Push *Allium* heads into the foam all around the rim of the vase, making sure there are no gaps between the flowers.

7 Wire up green lantern oranges or limes (see pages 12–15) and insert around the top of the *Allium* heads. Glue to further secure.

8 If the artichoke heads are dull in color, give them a very light spray of basil green paint, avoiding the purple tufts.

9 Insert a circle of artichoke heads at the top of the foam. Place a taller head in the center.

10 Push individual dark pink rose heads into the foam in the gaps at the base of the oranges.

A decorative glass candle holder brimming over with delphinium petals, and edged with tiny yellow rose heads.

Fill a jar with blue cornflower petals, to contrast gloriously with yellow rose heads.

In this example the jar is filled with *Allium* stems, but you could equally try fruit, pasta, assorted beans, cones, twigs, moss, or shells. Originally inspired by the limes, artichokes, and alliums, this arrangement is a sculptural design that can be adapted to suit your own taste. Dried red apple slices pick up the color from the deep pink roses, while two hanging rose heads are used to break up the long vase stem.

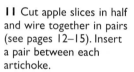

11 Cut apple slices in half and wire together in pairs (see pages 12–15). Insert a pair between each artichoke.

The use of a tall, glass container is a departure from more traditional dried flower holders. The colors and shapes of these dried plants are brought starkly forward by the lean, strong lines of a sphaghetti jar.

12 Pin light green reindeer moss in the gaps under the allium heads.

13 Cut off two rose heads, leaving a very short stem on each. Pierce the head with the end of some gold-coated wire. Wrap the short end around the stem and a little of the rest of the wire. Cut the wire so that a long length remains. Repeat with the second rose.

14 Insert the long end of each gold wire into the foam to create two staggered hanging flowers.

Tiered larkspur tin

Tin and enamel containers are always in plentiful supply in the form of buckets, pails, watering cans, troughs, and vases. Tin lives happily with unelaborate materials and designs, so a minimalist room with white walls, stainless steel, and glass, would be an excellent backdrop to this trough, the shape of which is very much reflected in the tiered larkspur arrangement. More spaced steps can be added to the basic design if you need more height, or try a combination of dark and light pink larkspur, with the white, as an effective color option.

Dark blue, pale blue, white larkspur, and lichen moss

YOU WILL NEED

- **Tin trough**
- **Dry florist's foam**
- **Knife**
- **Sphagnum moss**
- **22-gauge 12in (30cm) florist's wire**
- **Scissors**
- **Dark blue larkspur**
- **Pale blue larkspur**
- **White larkspur**
- **Lichen moss**

1 Cut dry florist's foam to fit the tin trough and sit level with the rim. Fix the foam in place and wedge smaller pieces into the gaps. Lightly cover the foam with sphagnum moss and pin in place (see pages 12–15).

2 Build up this display with three "blocks" of larkspur that form evenly spaced "steps." Push stems of dark blue larkspur into the foam to make a tall, rectangular block in the center of the arrangement, about five stems thick.

Give a candle a facelift with the simple addition of shells and lichen. An ideal decoration for a bathroom shelf.

3 Use a pair of scissors to trim away any wayward buds protruding from the top of the rectangle to form an even, flat shape.

4 Cut stems of pale blue larkspur, shorter than the dark blue larkspur. Insert these into the foam all around the dark blue larkspur rectangle. Keep the two larkspur blocks close together and aim for a fairly regimented look. The pale blue block should be about three rows thick. Do not insert the stems exactly one in front of the other, but stagger them to fill out the display.

It is not as easy to keep the distinct shape of the tiered sculpture, so it is important that you take the time to start the arrangement well and to create a solid first shape that you are happy with, since subsequent tiers will be built around it. Lichen moss is the ideal accompaniment to tin and larkspur, melding the colors to unite the whole design.

Larkspur is one of the most popular dried flower varieties, and it blends marvelously with tin. Always try to crop it when there are still one or two top buds left to open.

This chic arrangement is a classic combination of red roses with leaves, and moss. The fine cord plays to the silver of the square tin.

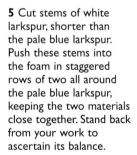

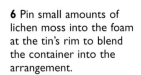

5 Cut stems of white larkspur, shorter than the pale blue larkspur. Push these stems into the foam in staggered rows of two all around the pale blue larkspur, keeping the two materials close together. Stand back from your work to ascertain its balance.

6 Pin small amounts of lichen moss into the foam at the tin's rim to blend the container into the arrangement.

Ceramic pot

This is a perfect design for the wonderful, trailing red *Amaranthus caudatus*, the ivory crackle-glazed pot being the perfect foil to its rich color and furry texture. Have a look around the home, in garden centers, florists, or craft shops for a similar classically shaped pot. If it is not decorated to your liking, experiment with your own paint effects or crackle glaze to achieve a unique finish.

Red *Amaranthus caudatus*

48

GLASS, WIRE, URNS, TIN, AND WOOD

YOU WILL NEED

- **Ceramic vase**
- **Newspaper**
- **Dry florist's foam**
- **Knife**
- **Sphagnum moss**
- **22-gauge 12in (30cm) florist's wire**
- **Scissors**
- **Eucalyptus**
- ***Achillea ptarmica* 'The Pearl' double**
- **Artificial burgundy berries**
- **Burgundy *Helichrysum***
- **Red *Amaranthus caudatus***
- **Damask rose dahlia**

1 Part fill the vase with crumpled newspaper. Fix dry florist's foam over the newspaper to sit 1in (2.5cm) proud of the rim. Pin sphagnum moss to cover the foam (see pages 12–15).

2 Wire up about 20 small bunches of eucalyptus leaves, two to three stems per bunch, using 22-gauge wire to bind the stems at their base (see pages 12–15). Choose long leaves to give the arrangement its wide collar.

Burgundy *Helichrysum* and damask rose dahlia

3 Insert the wired eucalyptus into the foam so that the leaves lie horizontally on the rim of the vase, forming a circle all around the base of the foam.

4 Wire up about eight small bunches of the achillea using three to four stems for each group. Insert these bunches, again working horizontally, immediately on top of the eucalyptus, evenly spaced all around the display.

5 Cut small berry stems away from a larger artificial stem and wire the cut stems, about halfway down, into groups of five (see pages 12–15). You will need about five bunches.

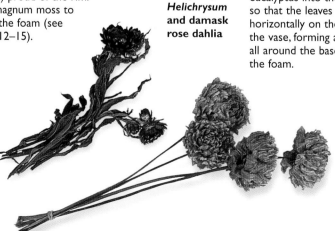

The red tones of this designer arrangement, from rose to burgundy and purple, and the texture of small sprigs of artificial burgundy berries, is set off by the ivory achillea, carrying through the pot color, with the wonderful green leaves of the eucalyptus forming a base.

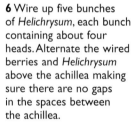

6 Wire up five bunches of *Helichrysum*, each bunch containing about four heads. Alternate the wired berries and *Helichrysum* above the achillea making sure there are no gaps in the spaces between the achillea.

A simple but effective design, this pot could stand alone in the center of a table, or be dramatically displayed on a tall pedestal.

7 Cut off the individual stems from a red amaranthus stalk and wire them into four bunches of about four to five stems each.

8 Insert the amaranthus evenly spaced, toward the arrangement base, pushing it in between the eucalyptus leaves.

9 To fill the top of the display, insert individual stems of dahlia. The finished arrangement should have a domed appearance.

Wirework stand

Stands can be found in all shapes and sizes and are useful for a buffet table display, enabling every inch of the table to be used for food rather than be taken up by a low arrangement. A vague thought of a pineapple with central leaves inspired this original design.

To keep a regular, graceful shape, it is a good idea to try to work in three sections, each filled with similar material. Your creation will evolve naturally but consider, as always, the key

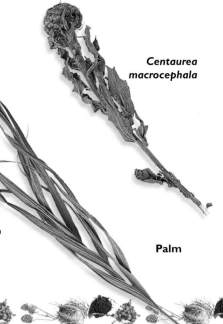

Centaurea macrocephala

Palm

YOU WILL NEED

- **Wirework stand**
- **Sphagnum moss**
- **Hydrangea**
- **Dry florist's foam**
- **Knife**
- **Binding wire**
- **Scissors**
- **22-gauge 12in (30cm) florist's wire**
- **Palm**
- **Pale blue larkspur**
- **White larkspur**
- **Cream *Celosia***
- **Artificial ivory and gold berries**
- **6 *Centaurea macrocephala***
- ***Nicandra***
- **Terracotta dyed achillea**
- **Light gray lavender**

1 Cover the base of a wirework stand with a thin layer of sphagnum moss. Position a ring of hydrangea heads around the edge of the bowl so that they can be seen through the wire.

2 Cut a square of dry florist's foam to fit inside the hydrangea ring and stand 2–3in (5–7.5cm) proud of the flowers.

3 Thread binding wire through the wire ring, over the foam, through the wire on the other side, and back over the foam. Twist the wire to secure and cut. Repeat to make a cross of wire over the foam.

4 Pin sphagnum moss all over the foam (see pages 12–15).

5 Insert about three palm stems centrally into the foam, so that they stand high, like a pineapple top.

6 Mentally separate the foam into three segments. Start by inserting about three stems each of pale blue and white larkspur, 3-4in (7.5-10cm) tall, in front of the palm in each third.

7 Insert individual stems to build up the display. Alternate blue and white larkspur at the base of the foam, above the hydrangea. Insert one or two cream *Celosia* heads in each third, between the two larkspur groups.

8 Insert one hydrangea in the middle of each section.

9 Cut smaller stems of ivory and gold berries from the main stem and wire into groups of two to four (see pages 12–15). Evenly distribute two groups in each third, at varying heights.

10 Remove the yellow flowers from six *Centaurea macrocephala* heads. Add a staggered pair to each third.

factors of surroundings, colors, texture, and proportions before you start designing.

Incorporate as much artificial fruit as you have available, such as grapes, pears, apples, and berries, especially if your fancy is for a Victorian feast arrangement. You could also create a similar fresh display, using fresh fruits in a variety of baskets.

If it proves difficult to find Nicandra *for this arrangement, try Chinese lanterns before they develop color, and palm can be substituted with strong flag leaf from wheat, grass, or Sorghum nigrum.*

11 Add stems of *Nicandra* in small groups at different levels. Stand back from your work to judge its balance. Fill in any final gaps with terracotta achillea.

12 Insert tall stems of lavender in front of the top larkspur.

13 Push a few leaves from the artificial berry stem in at the very bottom.

14 Bend a few palm leaves to make a loop and secure with wire. Insert two palm loops in each section, at different levels, to add further interest.

Fall basket

Nature provides us with a wonderful selection of creative material with which to work. This autumnal decoration enables tones of yellow, orange, brown, mahogany, green, and rust to blend together, keeping the colors of fall alive into winter.

Easy to display, and compact in its design, the basket sits comfortably in the kitchen among homemade bread, chutneys, and pickles. Alternatively, it could happily feature in a family room or richly decorated dining room.

Two-tone yellow and brown rose, and yellow achillea

YOU WILL NEED

- **Wooden basket**
- **Dry florist's foam**
- **Knife**
- **Binding wire**
- **Scissors**
- **Sphagnum moss**
- **22-gauge 12in (30cm) florist's wire**
- **Wheat, sprayed brown**
- **Terracotta dyed achillea**
- **2 lotus heads**
- **Yellow *Carthamus***
- **Golden zinnia**
- **Yellow achillea**
- **Craspedia**
- **Two-tone yellow and brown rose**
- ***Setaria italica***
- **Chinese lanterns**
- **Golden mushrooms**
- **Brown fatsia leaves**
- **Natural ting ting**

1 Cut a dry florist's foam block in half and fix centrally in the basket to stand 1in (2.5cm) proud of the rim (see pages 12–15).

2 Wrap binding wire around the handle level with the rim. Pass the wire over the foam, around the handle on the other side, and back over the foam. Twist the wire around the handle again and cut.

3 Pin in sphagnum moss pages 12–15).

4 Double leg wire (see pages 12–15) wheat stems and insert about ten groups of three to four stems evenly distributed all over the foam. You should still be able to pick up the basket by the handle.

5 Randomly add about six stems of terracotta achillea all over the foam.

6 Wire two lotus heads (see pages 12–15) and insert under the handle, pointing out in opposite directions.

7 Insert individual stems of yellow *Carthamus* in groups of three to four, close to each lotus and diagonally opposite each other.

The natural brown leaves can be collected during fall or winter country walks. Whether beech, ivy, oak, or fatsia leaves, they provide the perfect color background to the rich selection of oranges and yellows. Discard any imperfect leaves, and dry the rest thoroughly.

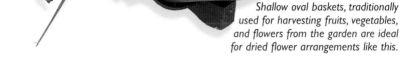

Shallow oval baskets, traditionally used for harvesting fruits, vegetables, and flowers from the garden are ideal for dried flower arrangements like this.

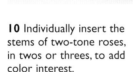

8 Wire four bunches each, three to four stems per bunch, of golden zinnia and yellow achillea. Evenly distribute the bunches over the foam, not forgetting the edges.

9 Add individual craspedia stems in groups of four or five. Stand back from the work and check for balance of color and material, making sure there are no noticeable blocks of a single color.

10 Individually insert the stems of two-tone roses, in twos or threes, to add color interest.

11 Add *Setaria italica* and a few Chinese lanterns to fill out the design.

12 Wire up four or five golden mushrooms (see pages 12–15) and push these in at random angles to add some texture.

13 Cut out sections of brown fatsia leaf and push a wire through each piece. Insert in the foam to curl around the basket.

14 Randomly add in a few stems of natural ting ting to add a little height and three-dimensional interest.

Wirework candle ring

Choose a suitable raised ring as your base, and enjoy sourcing dramatically colored and finished candles from specialist candle stores, garden centers, or gift shops. These aubergine candles were chosen to blend with dark red peonies to create a stunning centerpiece.

This is an opportunity to use water-preserved heather and treasured flower heads dried in silica gel, to add special interest (see pages 8–11). Any flowers dried with silica gel must be of the highest quality as the gel accentuates both the attractive and less agreeable aspects of a flower.

The wonderful steely blues of hydrangea, *Echinops*, and sea holly are perfect partners to the depth of the aubergine: a combination of colors found in so many richly colored fabrics.

YOU WILL NEED

- Raised wire ring
- Sphagnum moss
- Dry florist's foam
- Knife
- Binding wire
- Scissors
- 22-gauge 12in (30cm) florist's wire
- 3 aubergine candles, 2 in (5cm) diameter, 5in (13cm) high
- 3 dark red peony
- Hydrangea
- Dark blue lavender

- *Nigella damascena* 'Miss Jekyll Blue'
- *Echinops*
- *Eryngium planum*
- Dark red roses
- Green dyed eucalyptus
- Marjoram
- Lavender dyed *Gypsophila*
- Heather
- Green zinnia
- Wide, aubergine and gold voile ribbon

Green zinnia, dark red peony, and heather

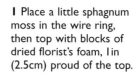

1 Place a little sphagnum moss in the wire ring, then top with blocks of dried florist's foam, 1in (2.5cm) proud of the top.

2 Thread binding wire through the wire ring, over the foam, and through the wire on the other side at regular intervals all around, to secure the foam. Twist around the wire to finish and cut.

3 Lightly cover the foam with sphagnum moss and pin in place (see pages 12–15).

4 Wire the candles (see pages 12–15). Push into the foam equidistant from each other.

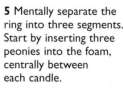

5 Mentally separate the ring into three segments. Start by inserting three peonies into the foam, centrally between each candle.

6 Individually insert hydrangea heads on the inside and outside edges of the foam; if the stems are weak double leg wire them first (see pages 12–15).

7 Add in small groups of material making sure each section looks roughly the same. Start with some dark blue lavender, *Nigella,* and *Echinops*.

8 Insert *Eryngium* and dark red roses around the candles. Randomly add in stems of eucalyptus, marjoram, *Gypsophila*, and heather. Stand back from your work frequently to judge the balance of color and material.

SAFETY
❀ Never leave a candle burning unattended, or let the candle burn down so low that the flame licks the dried flower material.

9 Add two green zinnia heads to each third, at different levels, to add a burst of color interest.

10 Fold a length of ribbon into a large bow and use 22-gauge wire to secure it in the middle (see pages 12–15). Make three bows and three extra tails. Insert a bow into the foam in front of each candle, and a tail behind.

To adapt this design for a Christmas centerpiece, add some gold ribbon, and complete the center with gilded cones, nuts, sumptuous fruits, and glossily wrapped sweets or mints.

Driftwood mirrors and photo frames

A wonderful project for young and old alike, a driftwood mirror can find a home in bedrooms, bathrooms, or holiday homes. Nature provides wonderful materials to choose from—a tapestry of textures that blend naturally together, so designing with them is easy. Lay a selection of ingredients before you, and be imaginative about what you choose.

An *Eryngium* 'Miss Willmott's Ghost' leaf and a coral branch

56

YOU WILL NEED
- **Small mirror**
- **Flat piece of driftwood, larger than the mirror**
- **Drill**
- **Rapid "Araldite" glue (if using outside) or glue gun**
- **Natural garden twine**
- **4 driftwood twigs**

Small amounts of:
- **Lichen moss**
- **Shells**
- *Eryngium* **'Miss Willmott's Ghost'**
- **Coral**
- **Xeranthemum**

1 Position a small mirror on a flat piece of driftwood and decide which edge is to be the top. Remove the mirror.

2 Drill two holes 2–2½in (5–5.5cm) apart on the top edge.

3 Glue the mirror in position on the driftwood.

4 Thread natural garden twine through the drilled holes, pull to desired length—to enable the mirror to be hung—and tie the ends in a knot at the back.

5 Glue four driftwood twigs of similar length to the driftwood base around the mirror, to hide the mirror edges, with the twigs at the short edges overlapping those on the long sides.

6 Collect small amounts of decorative material around you and try various arrangements at the top of the mirror.

7 When you find the right arrangement, glue the materials in place.

8 Form a bow from garden twine.

9 Glue the bow just under the top driftwood twig.

A garden twine bow

The finished driftwood mirror is ready to hang where it will evoke happy vacation memories.

Photo frames are similarly easy to personalize, as a gift or for one's own display. Frames can be found in all shapes and sizes, and you can use textured paints, verdigris kits, and gilt creams to change their appearance to suit the surroundings. The dullest of frames can be made to look a million dollars in just a few minutes.

With frames, it is a good idea to use flowers that keep their color well, and to choose materials that act as a backdrop to the photograph instead of dominating it. Cones and seed heads are ideal, as are dyed and sprayed materials. Try shells, moss, and driftwood for a look of the seashore, or press a few of your favorite blooms.

On this gilt rubbed frame (see pages 12–15), larch cones form a small nest at the ends of larch twigs at the bottom left corner.

The frame has been rubbed with gilt cream. Three cone pieces have been glued in a group in the left corner, with a few stems and small heads of Nigella orientalis, the heads positioned like buds on a stem. A few pieces of star anise were randomly added: the seed still in the anise adds extra interest. The same materials make up a smaller display top right.

This gilt rubbed frame, has green dyed Ruscus aculeatus and poppy pods of various sizes "growing" up the right side and along the bottom. A smaller group is glued on top left.

These ivory frames have been rubbed in places with a touch of gilt cream. The picture inside the oval frame is a simple glued arrangement of green oak leaves and tiny red broom bloom. At the bottom of the round frame an arrangement of red Gomphrena globosa, lavender, and small artificial gold berries has been glued on. A small corner arrangement on the square frame uses tiny green oak leaves, red Celosia, and red broom bloom.

DRIFTWOOD MIRRORS AND PHOTO FRAMES

A bundle of raspberry canes adorned with brown beechmasts, brown leaves, cream Gomphrena globosa, and a raffia bow.

Stalk bundles

Creating these stalk bundles will make you think twice before you fill the dustbin with the leftovers of other arrangements. There is great potential to be found with leftover *Cornus*, raspberry canes, grapevine, or wheat stalks. Keep dyed material ends too.

You can choose to make large bunches for a fireplace, smaller ones for a table center, or a tiny one for a charming gift. This bunch has been designed to sit with family photographs, on a side table, and the colors have been chosen to suit similar surroundings.

Red Cornus *prunings are an ideal base to set off pink* Gomphrena globosa *and burgundy berries.*

GLUE GUN IDEAS

YOU WILL NEED

- **Wheat stalks**
- **Scissors**
- **Garden twine**
- **Wide, dark green ribbon**
- **Glue gun**
- **Dark pink larkspur**
- **Wheat**
- **Binding wire**
- **6 'Mini' poppies**
- **Green dyed *Ruscus aculeatus***
- **2 pink zinnia heads**
- **Artificial burgundy berries**

1 Form a neat bundle of wheat stalks. Trim the ends so they are level, and tie tightly around the middle with garden twine.

2 Cover the twine with a length of ribbon and glue in place.

3 Tuck individual larkspur stems under the ribbon on either side and glue to secure. Position a few dark pink larkspur stalks the same length as the half bunch at either side of the ribbon.

The dark green ribbon picks up the green Ruscus *to set off the bundle.*

4 Glue in three staggered heads of wheat with the larkspur.

5 Form two small bows with single loops from more green ribbon (see pages 12–15).

6 Glue the bows to the ribbon on the bundle, centrally, close together on either side of the bunch.

7 Glue two groups of three poppies diagonally opposite each other on each side of the bunch. Add a few sprigs of green *Ruscus* all over.

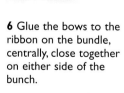

8 Glue two pink zinnia heads in the centers of the bows.

9 Pull a few stems of artificial burgundy berries away from the main stem and glue them throughout the bunch.

Artificial burgundy berry stem

Wheat stalks

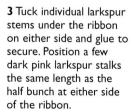

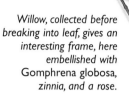

Red Cornus *stems cut down in early spring make an excellent deep red bow, here finished with cream* Santolina, zinnia, Ruscus, *and a rose.*

Bows

Creating with nature's natural waste offers endless opportunities for you to develop your own designs, using the natural curves, textures, and shapes available to you. Clematis provides yearly stems that can be shaped and prepared for use. When pruning, choose good-shaped, undamaged stems, form them into the bow shape, and leave to dry out naturally. Bows make natural, simple bases for a wall design, parcel dressing, or wedding pew ends. They also make inexpensive and beautifully personalized gifts.

Willow, collected before breaking into leaf, gives an interesting frame, here embellished with Gomphrena globosa, zinnia, *and a rose.*

YOU WILL NEED

- **Clematis twigs**
- **Reel of garden twine**
- **Scissors**
- **Dark green florist's spray paint (optional)**
- **Green dyed oak leaves**
- ***Nigella damascena* 'Miss Jekyll Blue'**
- **White *Gomphrena globosa***
- **5 burgundy roses**
- **Glue gun**
- **Wide, cream and gold hessian ribbon**
- **Binding wire**
- **Larch cones**

2 Form the other half of the bow and tie the center tightly with more twine. Shape out the bow. You can spray the bow green, as here, or leave it natural.

3 Take a few green oak leaves and tie the end of a reel of garden twine around the stems where the leaves finish. Do not cut the twine. Add about five staggered heads of *Nigella* evenly spaced and wrap twine around the stems.

4 Build up the small bunch by adding individual stems and winding the twine around them as you go, always in the same place. Add four to five staggered heads of white *Gomphrena* on the left, and five burgundy roses centrally. If you break a rose, simply glue it back in.

5 Cut the garden twine, leaving a tail to tie to the clematis, and tie it in a knot at the back. Trim stems to tidy.

6 Tie the bunch onto the clematis bow, slightly off center.

7 Fold a length of ribbon into a single bow and use binding wire to secure it in the middle. Glue the bow to the clematis at the bunch base.

8 Glue four to five small larch cones onto the bunch where needed.

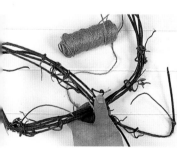

1 Tie three to four clematis twigs together with garden twine. Wind the clematis into half a bow, guided by how it naturally bends.

The elegant clematis bow will give a nostalgic feel to a bedroom wall.

Wall garden

Painting a picture with flowers is the theme of this garden. You can make similar but larger hangings based on houses and fields, rivers and ponds, or try a fence or gate. Variety of texture and shapes makes this an interesting display, as does attention to detail, and each garden you make becomes an original if you adapt it to your taste in colors and your own design.

Just as when planning a real garden border, think about shape, positioning tall flowers at the back, like trees, shorter flowers at the

White *Gomphrena globosa*

YOU WILL NEED

- **Basket base**
- **Glue gun**

Small amounts of:
- **Green reindeer moss**
- **Green dyed oak leaves**
- **Stones**
- **Lilac larkspur**
- **Carmine larkspur**
- **Red amaranthus**
- **Pink zinnia**
- **Cream** *Santolina*
- **Dark blue lavender**
- *Echinops*
- **Dark red rose**
- **Blue hydrangea**
- **Pink** *Celosia*
- **Palm**
- **Poppy (big pod)**
- *Achillea filipendulina* **'Moonshine'**
- *Achillea millefolium* **'Summer Pastels'**
- **Purple achillea**
- *Achillea ptarmica* **'The Pearl'**
- *Statice* **dumosa**
- *Nigella orientalis*
- *Nigella* **(green pod)**
- *Nigella damascena* **'Miss Jekyll Blue'**
- **White** *Gomphrena globosa*

1 Small amounts of material are glued onto the basket base to create a colorful and textured display. Start by gluing a few clusters of green reindeer moss around the bottom edge of the basket to begin the three-dimensional look. Add pairs of green oak leaves, randomly spaced, and a few firmly secured stones to resemble a pathway.

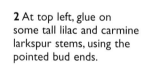

2 At top left, glue on some tall lilac and carmine larkspur stems, using the pointed bud ends.

3 Pull off two side shoots from the main red amaranthus stem. Glue these at the top, toward the right, to indicate the horizon.

Echinops

front, and a few seed heads nestled in like little treasures to be sought out. Why not also add a path and a moss lawn to complete the scene? Use this opportunity to press a few of your favorite garden flowers and add these as a focal point.

Basket arrangements have a timeless appeal, and flat basket shapes are readily available to buy. This themed blend of arresting color brings a year-round cottage garden into your home.

4 Put aside the zinnia, *Santolina*, lavender, *Echinops*, rose, and some of the hydrangea, for the front of the flower border, and the *Celosia*, palm, and poppy for later. Working from the top downward, position groups of the background plant material randomly all over the base to find an even balance of color, leaving some space for the bolder flowers. Glue the materials flat to the base.

5 Bring the pink zinnia in low into the picture to start building up a bolder look that brings the whole picture together.

6 Pull away small pieces from the main pink *Celosia* plume. Include three groups in the central plane of the picture.

7 Glue a few palm fronds top right, like a tree on the horizon. Group five stems of cream *Santolina* and lavender in the foreground.

8 Add a few *Echinops*, rose heads, a little hydrangea, and some poppy heads to fill the gaps and complete the garden. Take a few minutes to ensure that all the material is thoroughly glued in place, carefully adding more glue if necessary.

Harvest trug

A whole
pomegranate
and a grapefruit
slice

A traditional harvest trug has a natural, homespun feel, and the edging of fruits, flowers, and vegetables on this trug brings the abundance of harvest time into the home, carrying the warmth and colors of fall right through to winter.

Simple crossed-over bunches of natural wheat edge the basket, with orange *Carthamus* blended in to create the impression of strong thistles, and fruits and fungi summoning the bounty of harvest. The texture and boldness of corncobs is strongly marked against the straw color of their pale parchment husks. Beechmasts fill the center to the brim, their brown hues a contrast to the autumnal orange of the edges.

YOU WILL NEED

- *Zea mays* '**Harlequin**' **corncobs**
- **Scissors**
- **Trug**
- **Glue gun**
- **Wheat**
- **Garden twine**
- **Orange *Carthamus***
- **3 split oranges**
- **5 grapefruit slices**
- **2 pomegranates**
- **10 golden mushrooms**
- **Beechmasts**

Zea mays '**Harlequin**' **corncobs**

1 Remove a few pieces of husk from about five corncobs and flatten them out with your hands. Cut the husks in half.

2 Glue the half husks to the rim of the trug to completely cover it. Ensure the husks are well secured since they form the base to which everything else is added.

3 Tie eight bunches of wheat, about four to five heads each, with garden twine and trim the stalks to a manageable length. Glue crossed pairs of wheat bunches to the rim of the basket at the base of the handles and centrally at either end, heads facing outward.

4 Tie two generous bunches of orange *Carthamus* with twine and glue in the center of the wheat cross at each end.

5 Tease out the husks of eight whole corncobs, pulling some forward to create a pleasing, wild arrangement.

6 Firmly glue the corncobs in pairs on the trug's corners. Be fairly generous with the glue and hold the corncobs until secure.

Trugs, or similarly shallow rectangular-shaped baskets, are available in a variety of different materials. Adorning them in this way creates displays that will bring warmth and cheer to any part of the home.

The clean, Spartan lines of a trug are a wonderful offset to this profusion of fall colors and textures. This display could also be used to hold cutlery, breads, fruits, or pickle jars.

7 Glue a whole split orange to one side of the handle between the wheat and corn.

Beechmast

8 Cut two split oranges in half. Glue the two halves, cut side down, at either end with the *Carthamus*. Cut five grapefruit slices in half. Balance the opposite side of the whole orange with two half grapefruit slices.

9 Add a pomegranate, diagonally opposite, to two corners. Use more half grapefruit slices, in pairs, to fill. Add five pairs of golden mushrooms all around to balance and complete the display. Stand back to check all edges, inner and outer, and use a few orange *Carthamus* to fill any gaps.

10 Fill to the brim with beechmasts.

Seaboard ring

Bring the taste of summer beaches and salt sea air into your home with this spectacular ring. The essential black twig ring, or any similar basic structure, can be found in florists or craft stores.

You will have to allow yourself some time to collect the materials needed, but this is simply half the fun. Garden centers, bathroom stores, and aquarium suppliers are all excellent places to keep an eye out for interesting pieces of bark and driftwood, shells, seaweed, pebbles, corks, and moss.

The wealth of your collection will ultimately feature materials of varying shapes and sizes, and by following the basic principles of this project, you can make any number of rings. Don't be too methodical in your approach, aiming instead to create something original and personal to you.

YOU WILL NEED

- A 24in (60cm) black twig ring
- Silver birch bark
- Scissors
- Glue gun
- *Eryngium* 'Miss Willmott's Ghost'
- Skeleton leaves
- *Echinops*
- Statice dumosa
- *Centaurea macrocephala*
- Xeranthemum
- Blue reindeer moss
- Blue dyed coco moss
- Lichen moss
- Black moss
- Fir cones
- Driftwood
- A selection of shells, scallops, mussels, cockles, oysters, empty crab shells
- Pebbles
- Corks
- Shiny artificial beads (suggesting pearls)

1 Use a 24in (60cm) black twig ring as a basic frame.

2 Use scissors to cut a piece of silver birch bark into strips, no narrower than 0.5–2in (1–5cm).

3 Working on small sections of the ring at a time, glue on pieces of material. Add the materials randomly, but always with an eye to the even distribution of color and material. Concentrate on the sides of the ring as well as the center. Start with a few pieces of bark and heads of *Eryngium*.

4 Add a few skeleton leaves.

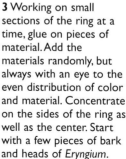

Lichen moss, a xeranthemum flower, and a stellatus shell.

6 As you come to the end of the ring, glue in the smallest pieces to fill gaps and add color interest where needed. Try adding a few broken pieces of shell.

7 Add a few shiny beads to give a pearly finish to reflect the light.

5 Keep trying various flowers, moss, leaves, cones, wood, shells, pebbles, and corks at different angles, in groups and alone. Plan a little ahead, then glue. Like a jigsaw puzzle, some pieces fit in and others don't. Try adding corks, cut in half lengthwise if necessary. Remember to balance the distribution of color and materials all around the design. Stand back from your work frequently to judge its balance and remove and reinsert materials where necessary. Hold the ring up to a wall to ensure it sits flat.

The seaboard ring houses a wealth of wonderful materials, evoking the sensual delights of sea foam and summer winds.

The oyster shell makes a wonderful container to nestle flowers in.

An enchanting pink stellatus shell is filled with statice dumosa, artificial berries, xeranthemum, and Eryngium 'Miss Willmott's Ghost.'

Herb and heart garland

Herbs are wonderful to work with, their natural colors and aroma providing a real feel-good factor wherever they are displayed. They also lend themselves to simple and natural arrangements. This is an original herb hanging for the kitchen or dining area.

The choice of herbs available to you is vast. Just save a few from your garden or kitchen pots to use in floral displays, and don't hesitate to use time-honored favorites such as mint, thyme, sage, and rosemary.

Hang the completed herb and heart garland wherever you will most appreciate the herbal scent it imparts.

YOU WILL NEED

- **Reel of garden twine**
- **Sage**
- **Sweet marjoram**
- **Bay**
- **Thyme**
- **Scissors**
- **Fabric, here a green check**
- **Needle and thread**
- **Oregano**
- **Thin rope, approx. 10ft (3m) long**

4 Fill the fabric hearts with oregano, not too packed in, and sew up the gap.

1 Tie the end of a reel of garden twine around a sage stem, about 2in (5cm) from the base. Do not cut the twine.

Thyme, sweet marjoram, bay, and sage

2 Add a stem each of marjoram, bay, and thyme. Tie neatly and cut the twine. Make three small bunches in the same way.

3 Cut out eight small fabric heart shapes: you could use a cookie cutter as a template. Sew each pair of hearts, right sides together, two-thirds of the way around. Turn the heart bags inside out.

5 Cut four 9in (23cm) lengths of rope and form into four loops, crossing over the rope ends. Attach each loop to a heart by sewing over the cross.

During the picking season you can make up garland rings of fresh herb varieties, then let them dry in a warm kitchen to carry the memory of summer days long into winter.

The small, check fabric hearts are simple to make and fill with your favorite scented herb, or you may prefer to hang gingerbread figures on the garland instead.

6 Cut three 10in (25cm) lengths of rope. Tie each rope around a herb bunch with a slip knot.

7 Lay out the remaining rope, then cut away two small lengths, large enough to make two bows. Tie the centers of the bows with twine.

8 Arrange the herb bunches and hearts around the main rope, ready to assemble.

9 Alternately thread a heart onto the main rope, followed by a bunch of herbs, and so on. Everything has been left loose on this garland, but you can fix the components to the rope with a stitch if you like. Tie a small bow to each end of the rope.

Sweet marjoram

Tied bouquet

A truly romantic posy can be held by an informal country bride, displayed on a dressing table or pine chest, or hung on the wall. Wherever it ends up, it takes with it a wonderful feel of charm and nostalgia. What can be more delicate and feminine than the frothy light heads of *Gypsophila* mingling informally with white *Nigella* in flower? The fragrance of white lavender sets the scene, and the simple design is tied with a generous lilac chiffon ribbon to complete the charming picture.

Nigella (green pod) in flower and lavender dyed Gypsophila

YOU WILL NEED

- **Lavender dyed Gypsophila**
- **White lavender**
- **Nigella in flower**
- **White Gypsophila**
- **Gypsophila 'Million Stars'**
- **Garden twine**
- **Scissors**
- **Lilac chiffon ribbon**

1 This bouquet is built up by inserting individual stalks into an arrangement held in one hand. As you work, aim to form a posy-shaped display, letting taller material sit in the center and positioning slightly shorter stems all around the sides. Remember that this arrangement is seen from all sides, so must be round and even, but not too regimented. Gather a posy of lavender dyed *Gypsophila*, keeping the material nicely spaced.

2 Add in stalks of white lavender, keeping an eye on the overall shape of the bouquet and ensuring an even distribution of material and color. The material should still not be too busy.

3 Add in stalks of *Nigella*. As always, check the bouquet for balance of material and color.

4 Position stalks of white *Gypsophila* all around the edge of the bouquet, just a little lower than the bulk of the material.

5 Use *Gypsophila* 'Million Stars' to form a band of color below the white *Gypsophila*, covering the still-visible stems.

6 Secure the completed bouquet by winding and tying garden twine around the stems at the position where the bouquet was held in the hand.

7 Use sharp scissors to cut all the stems below the tie, leaving enough length on the stalks to hold the bouquet comfortably.

Alternatively, collect frothy grasses and, perhaps, the seed heads of a clematis and the blue and mauve heads of *Nigella* in flower. Bring in a little marjoram, perhaps thyme, or the wonderful lime flowers of *Alchemilla mollis*. There are so many delicate, frothy, and perfumed materials to choose from and enjoy.

8 Wrap a length of ribbon around the garden twine and tie it in a knot.

A feature of so many dried flower displays, lavender has been used through the ages as an oil and a perfume.

9 Cut another long length of the ribbon and fold it into a large double bow. Use garden twine to secure the bow in the middle (see pages 12–15).

10 Position the bow on top of the knot of ribbon already in place. Take the right tail of the knotted ribbon over the front of the bow in the middle to cover the string. Pull it quite tightly over the bow then pass it to the back of the bouquet. Tie the ribbon tail at the back together with the other tail of the first ribbon.

The wispy froth of Gypsophila is an ideal companion to Nigella. The lilac chiffon adds the final touch to this misty bouquet.

Wall bunch

Wall bouquets can be made up in a huge variety of colors and styles, and their versatility means that they can be hung on a wall or laid on a blanket box.

Hops, and *Zea mays* 'Harlequin' corncob

This stylish bouquet has been designed with the kitchen in mind, using wheat and corns, majestic sunflowers, and subtle hops for a harvest feel. Gingham ribbon is a natural partner to this theme, and natural raffia picks up the color of the creamy corn husk. Simple, but very effective.

Sunflower

TIED ARRANGEMENTS

YOU WILL NEED

- **Dry or fresh bay**
- **Reel of garden twine**
- *Lepidium sativum*
- **Wheat**
- **Bearded wheat**
- **Yellow *Carthamus***
- **3 sunflowers**
- **3 yellow *Zea mays* 'Harlequin' corncobs**
- **22-gauge 12in (30cm) florist's wire**
- **Scissors**
- **Hops**
- **Wide, green gingham ribbon**
- **Raffia**

1 Hold a few long stems of bay in one hand. Tie the end of a reel of garden twine around the stems where the leaves end. Do not cut the twine.

2 Surround the bay, sides and back, with a few stems of *Lepidium sativum*, so that the *Lepidium* is taller than the bay at the back, and gets progressively shorter out to the sides. Take the garden twine in the other hand and wind it around the *Lepidium* and bay in the same place as before, to begin securing material.

3 To build up the bunch, add individual stems of material and wind the twine around the stems as you go, always in the same place. Place the bunch and the twine on a table as

you add materials. Work with taller materials centrally at the back and fan out shorter stems to the sides and front. The finished bunch should have a rough diamond shape. Add wheat to the right, bearded wheat to the left. Arrange yellow *Carthamus* in front of the *Lepidium,* and bearded wheat slightly to the left of center. Remember to keep binding tightly with the twine as you work.

4 Stagger three sunflowers down the display's center, pushing the stems individually into the bunch and binding around each one before adding the next.

5 Wire three corncobs (see pages 12–15) and bend the wires down toward the husk. Push the corn into the arrangement at the front and bind with twine.

6 Individually wire five to six hop stems using 22-gauge wire.

A stunning blend of golds and yellows set against rich green, this bouquet evokes long, hot summer days.

You do need to chose materials for a wall bunch carefully: long and flowing for the framework and dramatic for the center, such as the sunflowers used here. If your first attempt is not satisfactory, don't be discouraged, learn from your mistakes, and try again.

11 Take a handful of raffia and tie around the center of the length with a single raffia strand, again leaving long ends.

7 Push the hops into the bunch to fill out the sides, add interest, and disguise any unsightly stems. Bind as before.

8 Hold the bunch up to the wall, with the flowers pointing down, and make sure the sides and front look equally packed with material. Cut the garden twine and tie it in a knot at the back.

9 Fold a length of ribbon into a large double bow (see pages 12–15). Use a length of raffia to secure the bow in the middle, leaving long ends.

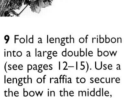

10 Position the bow over the twine binding so that the tails of the bow point toward the display. Tie the long raffia ends together at the back of the bunch.

12 Position the strands of raffia behind the loops of the bow so that the textured ends fall randomly down around the dried material. Secure the raffia bunch in place by tying the long ends of the single strand together at the back of the bouquet.

Stooks

There has to be a corner for a stook in every home, and for those favoring an up-to-date and informal arrangement, a tied stook is ideal. Although self-colored stooks are shown here, it is also possible to mix textures. Marjoram and roses, for example, mix well to create a totally different effect.

   You need a strong hand and a firm wrist to hold the material while you build it up. It is therefore a very good idea to be especially organized and to have your materials ready to hand.

The natural wheat stook is a simple design that fits naturally into any kitchen, adding a wonderful country feel.

TIED ARRANGEMENTS

YOU WILL NEED

- **Wheat**
- **Reel of natural garden twine**
- **Scissors**
- **Open-weave natural burlap**

Natural wheat stalks and open-weave natural burlap

1 Collect all your wheat in front of you and open it out into small bunches, about a handful each.

2 Take a handful of wheat and put the heads together, all at the same height. Tie the end of a reel of natural garden twine around the stems under the heads, leaving the reel attached.

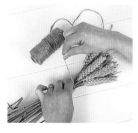

3 Add a few more heads of wheat at a time, binding them in tightly with the twine, always in the same place.

4 Add and bind more stems at a twisted angle and decreasing the height of the stalks. It is very important to keep the binding tight and not to put the stook down while constructing it.

5 As you add more twisted wheat, remember to grade the material down in height and always bind in one place. Pull in the stems tightly to achieve the look. Build up the stook so that it is even on all sides. When you are happy with the shape, cut the garden twine and tie it in a firm knot.

6 Cut the stems so the stook is the desired height. Don't cut too much off to begin with: it is easy to make the stook too short, but if it is too tall you can always cut more off.

7 Stand your stook up and trim again if necessary. Stooks that are forever falling over are irritating, so take time to get it right.

Generally, a successful stook is formed with tall, spiky material, rather than round heads. Don't be disappointed if you create some odd shapes when you first attempt a stook. There is a knack to be mastered, so persevere and the results will be enchanting.

A stook of marjoram finished with a lilac hessian bow is ideal as a kitchen display, and lavender stems form beautifully into a neat stook. A two-tone lavender voile makes a perfect bow.

8 Wrap a band of open-weave burlap around the stook and tie in a knot. Tie an extra length over the first burlap wrap to make two tails that hang loosely in front of the arrangement. Trim any material that stands proud or upsets the balance of the display.

Lilac larkspur is wonderfully colorful when bound as a stook with a two-tone lilac and lavender ribbon with gilt filigree. This display is fun for a side table or bedroom.

Light red roses, complete with their dried leaves, form a simple but elegant stook, finished with gold mesh.

The varying greens and browns of a Sorghum nigrum stook blend with a rustic green rope.

Tied arch

This project is unusual in concept, and a personal favorite of mine, probably because it does not have an overly structured feel. By creating an arch, a natural flow of flowers can be obtained to give a casual feel, as if two bunches have simply been picked at random and hung together.

The longer stems of larkspur and palm provide the free-flowing outline necessary to the creation of a tied bunch. Centrally, the rounded flowers are added to form interest, along with fatsia leaves and ribbons.

This project lets you into the secret of how easy it is to construct a stunning arch for your wall.

YOU WILL NEED

- **Palm**
- **Reel of garden twine**
- **Dark pink larkspur**
- **Dark blue larkspur**
- ***Nigella damascena* 'Miss Jekyll Blue'**
- **Craspedia**
- **Pink zinnia**
- **Scissors**
- **2 fatsia leaves**
- **Glue gun**
- **Wide, pink open-weave ribbon**
- **Wide, pink gingham ribbon**
- **Stem binding tape**
- **22-gauge 12in (30cm) florist's wire**

A fatsia leaf and palm leaves

Gingham ribbon, open-weave ribbon, and dark pink larkspur

1 Hold a few long stems of palm in one hand. Tie the end of a reel of garden twine firmly around the stems two-thirds of the way down. Do not cut the twine.

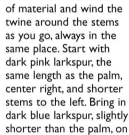

2 Add individual stems of material and wind the twine around the stems as you go, always in the same place. Start with dark pink larkspur, the same length as the palm, center right, and shorter stems to the left. Bring in dark blue larkspur, slightly shorter than the palm, on the right.

3 Add in shorter groups of *Nigella* centrally. Remember to ensure that all material is bound firmly in, but not so tightly that the stems break.

4 Add craspedia stems staggered down the length of the bunch. Bring in groups of pink zinnia just above the binding. Look carefully at the shape, checking, too, for balance of color and materials. Add a few more pieces of larkspur if needed. Cut the garden twine and tie it in a knot at the back of the bunch.

5 Trim the stems on an angle.

6 Repeat Steps 1–5 to make a second bunch, aiming to reverse the materials so that they will sit opposite the first bunch when the two are joined together.

7 Place the completed bunches on a flat surface and overlap the stems to form an arch as shallow or as deep as you wish. Wrap plenty of twine firmly around the stems where the bunches cross until the two bunches feel like a secure, single arch. Tie the twine tightly and cut.

8 Glue two fatsia leaves into the center of the arch, over the twine, along with a few craspedia and zinnia to tidy up the binding.

9 Form a single bow from pink open-weave ribbon and one from gingham ribbon (see pages 12–15). Glue the bows next to each other at the bottom edge of the center arch.

10 Wrap stem binding tape around a 22-gauge florist's wire and bend in half to form a hanger (see pages 12–15). Attach the hanger to the back of the arch.

TIPS

❀ Remember that the two bunches should almost be mirror images of each other. With this in mind, it is a good idea to divide the material into two piles as you use it, so you have enough for both bunches.

❀ Working on a tabletop will help you to keep the bunches flat at the back.

A red brick alcove provides an ideal backdrop to the tied arch. The bricks' hues blend with the arrangement's pinks while throwing forward the stronger blues and yellows.

Wired, double, and square topiary

On a visit to the garden center you will find a wide variety of topiary frames, some round, square, or pyramid shaped, or in the form of animals and birds. All make ideal bases for dried topiary sculptures.

  With only a glue gun and a large selection of plant material—and a lot of patience—you can create a wonderful topiary shape. It seems natural to use one single material for each design, but a mix will of course work, although tall, spiky materials should be avoided since they do not easily take on the shape of the topiary frame.

Wired topiary

An architectural topiary, like this pyramid, can look stunning in the most modern of settings, giving a contemporary, sculptured look.

YOU WILL NEED

- **Pyramid wire topiary frame**
- **Black moss**
- **Glue gun**

1 Starting at the base of a topiary frame, firmly glue on pieces of black moss, leaving no frame showing. Treat this arrangement like a jigsaw puzzle, finding the right piece of moss to fit a specific gap.

2 Glue on more moss, working systematically up the frame. Overlap the moss pieces and aim to keep the material fairly flat to the frame.

3 When you have reached the top, stand back to check for gaps and fill if necessary.

Wired topiaries like this go well with the lean, elegant lines of minimalist interior decorations.

Double topiary

Positioned on a dresser a double topiary tree is a classic. Make two or more matching trees in different sizes and stand them together for maximum impact.

YOU WILL NEED

- **Cane, stick, or twig to use as a trunk**
- **Pruning shears**
- **Glue gun**
- **Plant pot or other container**
- **Dry florist's foam**
- **Knife**
- **Cement, plaster of Paris, or nylon reinforced plaster**
- **Binding wire**
- **Sphagnum moss**
- **22-gauge 12in (30cm) florist's wire**
- **Sphagnum moss**
- ***Nigella orientalis***

1 Cut a suitable trunk for the tree to about 13in (32cm) long. If your stick is quite thin, use two together, as here.

2 Glue the trunk to the base of a container and wedge it in with chunks of florist's foam.

Once the base and stem of the topiary tree are secure, the rest will follow easily.

3 Pour cement or plaster of Paris into the pot around the trunk, using the manufacturer's guidelines. Or push in nylon reinforced plaster if using a small pot. Leave to set.

To bring out the vibrant color of the Chinese lanterns, you could spray a little orange florist's paint over the completed tree.

Double and treble topiaries are challenging to construct, but well worth the effort. This stunning double tree is 15in (38cm) tall. To make anything larger it is advisable to use whole foam spheres of varying sizes. This double tree is covered with *Nigella orientalis*, and could easily be sprayed dark green or gold at different times of the year. Whatever you cover your tree with, remember to source a plentiful supply of material, as it always takes more than you imagine to complete.

The square topiary is a fun design and easy to construct, ideal for getting young fingers enmeshed in a challenge. You could also make the tree in a square plant pot, to accentuate the angularity.

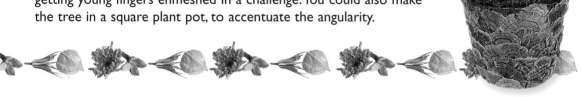

77

WIRED, DOUBLE, AND SQUARE TOPIARY

4 Cut two blocks of florist's foam, one 3in (7.5cm) square and the other 2¼in (6cm) square. Push the smaller block firmly and centrally onto the top of the trunk, and secure with glue.

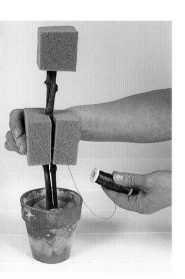

5 Cut the larger foam block in half. Hold the two halves on either side of the trunk, halfway up, and secure with glue. Wrap binding wire around the blocks to secure them firmly to the trunk.

6 Pin a thin layer of sphagnum moss over the foam (see pages 12–15).

7 Cut stems of *Nigella orientalis* to about 1in (2.5cm) and individually insert them into the foam. Start working at the base of the top block—it is difficult to cover this area at the end—pushing in close to the foam.

8 Insert the stems into the top of the bottom block next. Work your way all around the tree, keeping the *Nigella* heads level.

9 When completed, glue moss to the cement at the base to cover.

Square topiary

To keep the square shape, this technique uses a glue gun to stick petals to a foam square pierced on a trunk, instead of inserting stems of material into the foam core.

YOU WILL NEED

- **Cane, stick, or twig to use as a trunk**
- **Pruning shears**
- **Glue gun**
- **Plant pot or other container**
- **Dry florist's foam**
- **Cement, plaster of Paris, or nylon reinforced plaster**
- **3in (7.5cm) square of dry florist's foam**
- **Binding wire**
- **Scissors**
- **Chinese lanterns**
- **Green reindeer moss**

1 Choose a trunk for the tree and cut or saw to size.

2 Glue the trunk to the base of a container and wedge it in with chunks of florist's foam.

3 Pour cement or plaster of Paris into the pot around the trunk, following the manufacturer's instructions, or push in nylon reinforced plaster if using a small pot. Leave to set.

4 Push a square of florist's foam firmly and centrally onto the trunk, and secure with glue.

5 Wrap binding wire around the trunk at the base of the foam square, then wrap it over the foam and back around the trunk. Repeat a few times.

6 Cut or tear Chinese lantern heads into sections. Glue these onto the foam square, starting from underneath and moving round the square. Overlap the rows of material and remember to cover over the edges of the square.

7 Glue green reindeer moss to the cement at the base to cover.

Traditional topiary spheres

You can easily create sculptural, trimmed, and shaped topiaries in all types of material once you have grasped some basic principles. Patience and time are the most important necessities of successful topiary design. It is easy to underestimate how long a topiary will take, and it is never a good idea to rush, and risk losing the arrangement's distinctively even shape.

YOU WILL NEED

- **Dry florist's foam sphere**
- **Knife**
- **Cane, stick, or twig to use as a trunk**
- **Pruning shears or saw**
- **Plant pot or other container**
- **Glue gun**
- **Dry florist's foam**
- **Cement, plaster of Paris, or nylon reinforced plaster**
- **Binding wire**
- **Scissors**
- **Sphagnum moss**
- **22-gauge 12in (30cm) florist's wire**
- **Craspedia**
- **Yellow reindeer moss**

1 Cut a dry florist's foam sphere in half.

2 Choose a trunk for the tree and cut or saw to size.

3 Glue the trunk to the base of a container and wedge it in with chunks of florist's foam.

4 Pour cement or plaster of Paris into the pot around the trunk, following the manufacturer's instructions, or push in nylon reinforced plaster if using a small pot. Leave to set.

5 Push the half sphere firmly and centrally onto the trunk, and secure with glue.

6 Wrap binding wire around the trunk at the base of the half sphere, then wrap it over the foam and back around the trunk. Repeat a few times to give the head the necessary strength and security to hold the materials added to it.

7 Cover the foam with a thin layer of sphagnum moss and pin in place (see pages 12–15).

8 Cut craspedia stems to about 1in (2.5cm) and individually insert them into the foam, starting at the top and keeping tight to the foam. Use smaller heads at the top and larger ones around the base.

9 Glue yellow reindeer moss to the cement at the trunk base, and beneath the tree head, to cover.

A wonderful cerise, velvety Celosia tree, displayed in a golden urn with gold mesh ribbon.

A cheerful craspedia tree on a gnarled vine stem, in a container bound with raspberry cane and twine.

These wired hydrangea petals loosen the usually rigid circular shape of a sphere topiary.

Craspedia and yellow reindeer moss

Topiary spheres look great on their own as a stunning feature. Try a stylish pair on the mantelpiece or to dress a dinner table. Then use them again, perhaps as a feature in the hallway.

All kinds of containers, whether plain or decorated terracotta pots, shaped or textured pots, can be used as the base of a topiary.

A pot covered in hydrangea petals is topped by a topiary of Nigella orientalis 'Transformer.' Green reindeer moss covers the cement.

A small gold urn and a few gold pebbles provide a suitable base for a pink Gomphrena topiary.

A topiary of statice dumosa blossom fills a pot rubbed with gilt cream (see pages 12–15). Black moss covers the cement.

This rusty bucket sets off the velvety cerise Celosia topiary.

Oak tree

The oak tree in this arrangement induces the feeling of fall: berries, fruits, cones, and open log fires crackling in the grate. It is a naturally sophisticated and comforting look to nestle with baskets and gingham. This tree can be made to any size specification, and gives a wonderfully warm welcome to an entrance hall or family room. The trimmings can be removed at Christmas and the tree sprayed gold and decorated with festive trimmings for a yuletide feel.

Cinnamon sticks, wired and guttered rose hips and acorns.

TOPIARY TREES

YOU WILL NEED

- **Dry florist's foam sphere**
- **Knife**
- **Thick grapevine to use as a trunk**
- **Saw**
- **Stones**
- **6in (15cm) terracotta pot**
- **Cement or plaster of Paris**
- **Glue gun**
- **Binding wire**
- **Scissors**
- **Sphagnum moss**
- **22-gauge 12in (30cm) florist's wire**
- **Dried apple slices**
- **Stem binding tape**
- **Cinnamon sticks**
- **Dried rose hips**
- **Strictum cones**
- **Acorns and cups**
- **Natural oak leaves**
- **Long twigs, not straight**
- **Brown coco moss**

1 Cut a dry florist's foam sphere in half.

2 Saw a grapevine to the desired height. Pour stones into the base of a terracotta pot as ballast, then position the vine centrally in the pot. Pour cement or plaster of Paris into the pot around the vine, following the manufacturer's guidelines. Leave to set.

3 Push the foam half sphere firmly and centrally onto the trunk and secure with glue.

4 Wrap binding wire around the trunk at the base of the half sphere then wrap it over the foam and back around the trunk. Repeat a few times to give the head the necessary strength and security to hold the materials added to it.

5 Cover the foam with a thin layer of sphagnum moss and pin in place (see pages 12–15).

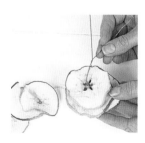

6 Wire up pairs of apple slices—choose red apples so the peel is colorful—then gutter them (see pages 12–15).

7 Break cinnamon sticks in half, or leave whole. Wire up the cinnamon sticks at the ends and gutter (see pages 12–15).

8 Chose rose hips with stems, wire them into groups of three to four hips, and gutter.

9 Wire up and gutter strictum cones (see pages 12–15), acorn, and cups.

Dried apple slices

The autumnal oak tree has a wilder look than traditional topiary spheres.

10 Insert separate oak leaves firmly into the foam sphere. If necessary you can double leg wire the leaves (see pages 12–15). Cover the whole tree, creating a balanced, round shape. Stand back and regard the tree from all angles.

11 Randomly add in twigs that are taller than the oak leaves, for a wild look.

12 Add in the wired cones in groups of two or three. Insert pairs of cinnamon sticks, small groups of acorns and hips, and the pairs of apple slices. Make sure the materials are evenly spaced around the tree.

13 Glue brown coco moss to the cement at the base to cover.

Spiral topiary

This spiral tree is impressive and dramatic, and while the technique of making it is not difficult, it does require considerable time and patience.

A spiral topiary can give height to a confined space when made tall and thin, or the thickness and height can be altered to create a shorter, wider design if preferable. Start the design with the tree's location in mind. One tree can perhaps fill a vacant corner, or a pair can stand dramatically either side of a fireplace. In a bare room this tree can provide an architecturally stunning display.

Bunch of orange tagetes

YOU WILL NEED

- **24in (60cm) length of straight vine or wood**
- **Hammer**
- **Nail**
- **Stones**
- **6½ in (16cm) plant pot**
- **Cement or plaster of Paris**
- **Sphagnum moss**
- **Chicken wire, 7 x 37in (18 x 94cm)**
- **Binding wire**
- **Scissors**
- **Staple gun or small nails**
- **Glue gun**
- **Orange tagetes**

1 Hammer a nail into the top of a vine to secure the spiral to. Pour stones into the base of a plant pot as ballast, then position the vine in the pot, left of center, not too close to the edge. Pour cement or plaster of Paris into the pot around the vine, following the manufacturer's guidelines. Leave to set.

2 Place handfuls of moss on a length of chicken wire and neatly roll up to form a snake that is thicker at one end and gets gradually thinner toward the other.

3 Bend over the wire at each end and sew up the edges with a little binding wire until no sharp wires are left sticking out.

4 Use more binding wire to tie the thin end of the wire and netting snake onto the nail in the vine. Form the snake into a spiral around the vine and use a staple gun or small nails to secure the snake to the vine in the middle area and at the base—the snake must be especially secure at the bottom.

Many materials are suitable for use on a spiral topiary: round flowers, flat moss, pebbles, shells, seed heads, and foliage, amongst others. Whatever you choose, make sure you have a plentiful supply to complete the whole tree as it is easy to underestimate how much you need.

The secrets of enjoying the creation of this tree are to plan in advance and allow yourself plenty of time. If you don't succeed at first, do try again. It will be worth it.

The rich textured tagetes of this dramatic spiral topiary tree contrast well with the tree's fashionable rusty container.

5 Starting at the base, glue individual orange tagetes heads onto the spiral. Take your time, ensuring that the material is nicely packed together so that no gaps appear.

6 Keep gluing flowers around the spiral. Make sure you cover the underside as well as the top. The tree will be viewed from all angles.

7 When you have glued tagetes all over, stand back and look for gaps from all angles. Add more flowers if necessary. If the tagetes look at all uneven you can trim the whole tree carefully with scissors.

8 Glue moss to the cement at the base to cover.

Floor-standing hydrangea tree

A somewhat advanced project, this large, floor-standing hydrangea tree looks stunning in any setting. Be confident when deciding to try this project, and remember speed comes with practice, so don't lose heart when it doesn't evolve quickly. Hydrangea dries in so many shades, and if you can collect together a range of colors in the late fall that blend together, they will look wonderful. You need a considerable number of heads, so collect plenty while they are available, but do leave them until late in the season to dry properly.

   The stems of the tree have been chosen carefully to bring in a sense of movement to the arrangement, and any combination of foam sphere sizes can be used, depending on the size and shape of your trunks. Chose your wood first and the sphere decision will be made for you; the trunk will dictate the best sphere to use.

YOU WILL NEED

- **Interesting, thick, strong sticks to use as trunks**
- **Saw**
- **Stones**
- **12in (30cm) terracotta pot, or a plastic pot that can be put into a slightly larger terracotta pot**
- **Cement or plaster of Paris**
- **Glue gun**
- **8in (20cm) dry florist's foam sphere**
- **7in (18cm) dry florist's foam sphere**
- **6in (15cm) dry florist's foam sphere**
- **Binding wire**
- **Scissors**
- **Sphagnum moss**
- **22-gauge 12in (30cm) florist's wire**
- **Hydrangea heads**
- **Pebbles**
- **Newspaper**
- **Gold florist's spray paint**

1 Choose a number of suitable trunks and saw to size.

2 Pour stones into the base of a large terracotta pot as ballast, and position the trunks in the pot. Pour cement or plaster of Paris into the pot around the trunks, following the manufacturer's guidelines. Leave to set. If you are worried that a terracotta pot will crack, use a plastic pot to cement in.

A dried hydrangea head

3 Aim to push on and cover one sphere before going onto the next. Depending on the strength and arrangement of your trunks, you would usually position the largest foam sphere on the highest trunk, and the smallest on the shortest trunk. Push a sphere firmly onto the trunk and secure with glue.

4 Wrap binding wire around the trunk at the base of the sphere then wrap it over the foam and back around the trunk. Repeat a few times to give the head the necessary strength.

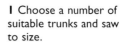
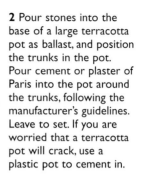
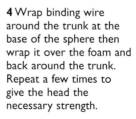

Hydrangeas tone beautifully with wooden floorboards. Here the rush chair seat adds further interest as it blends in with the buttermilk walls and pine skirting.

5 Pin a thin layer of sphagnum moss over the foam (see pages 12–15).

6 Depending on the size, either use the whole hydrangea head or divide it into florets. Individually push hydrangea stems into the foam, or double leg wire the stems first (see pages 12–15).

7 Keep adding hydrangea heads all over the sphere, keeping them close to the foam.

8 Repeat Steps 3–7 for each foam sphere.

9 Look critically at the tree and replace or replenish hydrangea heads as required. Remember to check the tree from all angles.

10 Lay some pebbles on newspaper or scrap paper and spray with gold florist's spray paint, following the manufacturer's guidelines. Place a layer of natural pebbles on top of the cement in the pot and sprinkle the gold pebbles on top to finish.

Mossed pot pourri basket

This pot pourri basket is a simple and inexpensive idea, and quick to create. Based on roses and lavender, the small bunches have a feminine feel, evoking cottages, pine, and lace. Choose a basket with an open weave to enable the rim to be mossed easily. As always, choose quality flowers as small amounts need to be especially beautiful. One exquisite rose can suffice, so cut a few of your favorite perfumed roses and dry them carefully.

Reel of gauze ribbon

YOU WILL NEED

- **Small decorative basket with handle**
- **Binding wire**
- **Scissors**
- **Sphagnum moss**
- **Cream feverfew**
- **Lavender**
- **Dark pink roses**
- **Garden twine**
- **22-gauge 12in (30cm) florist's wire**
- **Narrow, pink voile ribbon**
- **Glue gun**

Pot pourri, dark pink rose, lavender, and cream feverfew

1 Cut a long length of binding wire. Thread one end of the wire through the weaving of the basket rim and twist to secure.

2 Place a handful of sphagnum moss on the rim of the basket. Wrap the binding wire over the moss and thread it back through the weaving to secure it in place.

3 Continue binding more moss, leaving a gap of about 1in (2.5cm) between binds. Attach

more wire as you need it When you arrive back at the start, wrap the end of the wire in the weaving a few times and cut.

4 Make two small bunches of dried material of varying heights, holding the plants in one hand while adding material with the other. Position cream feverfew at the back, lavender stems in front, and three or four dark pink roses, with the thorns removed, down the center, so that all the material is staggered. Secure the bunches just below the blooms with garden twine.

5 Trim the stems of both bunches, leaving enough stalk to handle the bunches comfortably.

Collect petals and small flower heads and dry them separately, well in advance, ready to make your own pot pourri. Try to stick to a color scheme that suits your home, whether lavender and roses, or cinnamon and orange.

An enduring display for the kitchen or bedroom, the combination of rose, lavender, and cream feverfew is difficult to beat.

9 Glue each bow over the stems of the dried material, covering the wire and twine on each.

6 Position one bunch of material on the mossed rim of the basket, by the handle, with the stems closest to the handle and the blooms fanning out over the moss where they can be seen. Thread the florist's wire through the weaving under the stems and wrap it around the stems to secure them. On the basket's inside, twist the wire ends together, cut the loose ends, and thread what is left back into the weaving to hide the mechanics.

7 Attach the second bunch on the opposite side of the basket in the same way.

8 Form a double bow of ribbon and use binding wire to secure it in the middle (see pages 12–15). Make another bow in the same way.

10 Fill the completed basket to the top with the pot pourri of your choice.

Heart

Hearts always have a place in our lives, not only on Valentine's and wedding days. This basic shape can be filled out in many ways and used as an adornment in a bedroom or a quiet corner of the home, as a gift, or to dress a parcel. Look around for wicker, tin, and wire hearts, all inspirational to work with. This lavender heart is a classic design, built around a wreath ring bent into shape. It can be left unadorned or decorated with a simple green or gold leaf (see pages 12–15). Twigs and red roses are other natural companions.

Dried lavender

YOU WILL NEED

- **10in (25cm) flat wire wreath ring**
- **Reel of binding wire**
- **Sphagnum moss**
- **Lavender**
- **22-gauge 12in (30cm) florist's wire**
- **Scissors**
- **Glue gun**
- **Green stem binding tape**
- **Lichen moss**

2 Gently bend the center wires at top and bottom downward to form a heart shape.

4 Take a bunch of about 20 lavender stems and slightly stagger the heads. Cut a 22-gauge 12in (30cm) florist's wire in half. Make a double leg bunch (see pages 12–15) and trim the ends so that the final stems measure about 4in (10cm) from the head to the base of the stalks. Make about 50 bunches in the same way.

1 Take a flat 10in (25cm) wreath ring and hold it with a strut at the top.

3 Secure the end of a reel of binding wire to the back of the frame. Take a handful of sphagnum moss and position it on top of the frame. Bind the moss in place by winding around it with the binding wire, leaving a gap of about 1in (2.5cm) between binds. Try to hold the reel at an angle, so that the binding does not fall straight across the moss. Continue binding more moss to the heart frame, keeping the moss even. When you return to the start, leave the reel of wire attached.

5 Start binding the lavender bunches over the moss heart. Place the first bunch on top of the moss with the flower end pointing to the center of the heart. Use the still secured reel of wire to wind around the lower part of the lavender stems to secure the first bunch.

The arrangement's moss base can also be used on its own. Here, a single lavender bunch is tied in with a few red roses and the mechanics covered with a double bow of Shaker blue gingham, retaining the simple look. You could also spray the moss gold for a radically different finish.

Red roses are a classic contrast to the blue of lavender.

8 Trim and secure the binding wire at the back of the heart. Bend a 22-gauge wire wrapped with stem binding tape in half to form a hanger and secure it to the back of the heart around the frame and moss (see pages 12–15). Glue lichen moss to the back of the heart to hide the wire mechanics.

The silver heart (above) is created from twisted galvanized wire with a lavender and rose ornamentation and silver thread. The contrasting gold heart (right) has been made with tiny gilded pittisporum leaves (see pages 12–15) glued onto the wire shape and tied with gold thread.

Hang this lavender heart on the wall to bring romance to your bedroom.

6 Lay subsequent lavender bunches flat on the heart, slightly overlapping and staggering from left to right, then filling in with a central bunch. Bind each bunch firmly in, keeping all the wire on top and covering it with the following bunches. Hold the wreath against the wall at regular intervals to check its overall shape.

7 When you return to the beginning, wire as far as possible, then use a glue gun to attach the final bunches—you may need to make the last bunch shorter than previously.

Alchemilla mollis and salmon *Helichrysum*

Mantel swag

Mantel swags can be used in many locations. Here, chili peppers and lantern fruits provide the finishing touches. Dry chili peppers, in all their colors, can be brought into many designs, including chili wreaths, trees, and garlands. If a twig plait is not available, try straw plaits, or bunch several raspberry or garden canes together for a strong base.

The choice of ribbon can have a dramatic impact on an arrangement, changing it from a wistful country design to a more classical, sophisticated statement. Allow yourself plenty of time to enjoy yourself, and do get into the habit of clearing your workspace regularly.

WIRED ARRANGEMENTS

YOU WILL NEED

- **22-gauge 12in (30cm) florist's wire**
- **Scissors**
- ***Alchemilla mollis***
- **Salmon *Helichrysum***
- ***Nigella orientalis* 'Transformer'**
- **Red broom bloom**
- **Yellow *Santolina***
- **Orange *Carthamus***
- **Green amaranthus**
- **Twig plait**
- **Reel of binding wire**
- **Glue gun**
- **Sphagnum moss**
- **Chili peppers**
- **2 green lantern oranges or lantern limes**
- **Wide, lime green voile ribbon**
- **Stem binding tape**

1 Wire up plenty of bunches of five to ten stems each of *Alchemilla*, salmon *Helichrysum*, *Nigella*, red broom bloom, yellow *Santolina*, orange *Carthamus*, and green amaranthus (see pages 12–15).

2 Wrap the end of a reel of binding wire around the end of the twig plait a few times. Do not cut the wire.

3 Choose a bunch of long material to start the swag. Position the bunch and wrap around the stems, fairly low, with the binding wire.

4 Continue securing bunches to the left, right, and center of the arrangement by overlapping the stems and binding with wire. As you lay each new bunch, put a bunch of the same material aside to use later at the other end.

5 Add material until you reach the center of the plait. Place the plait against a wall regularly to make sure it sits flat and that the materials are evenly distributed throughout.

6 Secure the binding wire, and wind to the other end,

7 Repeat steps 2–5, working from the other end of the plait to the middle, using the material in roughly the same order. Bring the final bunch as close as possible to the previous central bunch. Secure the binding wire and cut.

The green of the Nigella, amaranthus, and Alchemilla are the perfect complement to the salmon Helichrysum and orange Carthamus in this sweeping display.

8 Glue sphagnum moss over the stems in the middle.

9 Choose two branches of chili peppers with plenty of heads, and wire each one.

10 Glue chili bunches at intervals throughout the swag.

11 Wire up two green lantern oranges or lantern limes (see pages 12–15). Glue the oranges onto the moss in the middle of the swag so that they are central and will be seen from below the arrangement when it is on the wall.

12 Fold a length of ribbon into a double bow and use 22-gauge wire to secure it in the middle (see pages 12–15). Make an extra pair of tails. Glue the tails and then the ribbon in the center of the swag, by the oranges.

13 Gutter a 22-gauge florist's wire and bend in half to form a hanger (see pages 12–15). Make a second hanger and attach one to each end of the plait, at the back.

Chili peppers

Orange Carthamus

Bunched bowl

Plan this technique in advance: it is surprisingly demanding so take time and have confidence in your ability. Enjoy finding the right container as it is important if you are to achieve stunning results.

There are so many secrets of this trade, and one is definitely not to underestimate the uses for the huge variety of mosses available—black moss, reindeer, and coco to name but a few. Here, gray lichen moss makes an essential basket filler and provides the perfect

Dark red rose, *Eryngium* **'Super Nova', and artichoke**

YOU WILL NEED

- **Wire bowl**
- **Dry florist's foam**
- **Knife**
- **Binding wire**
- **Scissors**
- **Lichen moss**
- **Small stones, some natural, some sprayed gold**
- **22-gauge 12in (30cm) florist's wire**
- **Red amaranthus**
- *Nigella damascena* **'Miss Jekyll Blue'**
- **Marjoram**
- *Eryngium* **'Super Nova'**
- **Glue gun**
- **Dark red rose**
- **Artichokes**
- **Dark green florist's spray paint**
- **White candle, 2in (5cm) diameter and 12in (30cm) high**
- **Barbecue skewers or cocktail sticks**
- **Anchor tape**

1 Cut a square of dry florist's foam to fit the base of the wire bowl and sit 1–2in (2.5–5cm) below the rim.

2 Wrap binding wire around a wire rung a third of the way down the bowl. Pull the wire over the foam, wrap it around a rung on the other side, and back over the foam. Twist to secure the wire. Repeat to make a cross of wire over the foam.

3 Sprinkle lichen moss into the bowl all around the foam, no higher than the block. Drop in some natural and gold stones that can be seen from the outside.

Lichen moss

4 Wire several bunches of plant material, wrapping the wire around the middle of the stems and keeping the wire ends at right angles to the bunches (see pages 12–15). Make bunches of single blooms or mixed using red amaranthus, *Nigella*, and marjoram, making sure about half the bunches contain one or two blue *Eryngium* heads.

5 Attach a bunch to the rim of the bowl by wrapping the 22-gauge wire around the wire of the bowl, positioning the bunch so the stems point in and the flowers point out.

6 Alternate bunches with and without the *Eryngium*, making sure the blue can be seen, until the rim is covered.

backdrop and contrast to the dark red and steely blue flowers. It also nestles in to neaten around the candle base. Alternatively, you could use hydrangea, cones, pebbles, or shells.

The striped burgundy *Nigella* carries the red color from rose to amaranthus, with the stems of marjoram providing a flowing edge to complement the artichokes.

This design will add a touch of elegance and sophistication to a sideboard or dining room table. There are many species of Eryngium available, or Echinops can be used as an alternative.

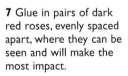

SAFETY

✿ Never leave a candle burning unattended, or let the candle burn down so low that the flame licks the dried flower material.

7 Glue in pairs of dark red roses, evenly spaced apart, where they can be seen and will make the most impact.

8 If the artichoke heads are particularly pale, give them a very light spray of dark green paint, avoiding the purple tufts (see pages 12–15).

9 Individually insert artichoke stems into the foam through the sides of the wire bowl, just below the rim. Insert one large, or two small ones, at regular intervals but at different angles.

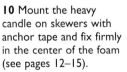

10 Mount the heavy candle on skewers with anchor tape and fix firmly in the center of the foam (see pages 12–15).

11 Check the rim for gaps and glue in small amounts of material to fill. Glue lichen moss over the foam to cover.

Wreath

To create this peaceful, elegant cream and green door wreath, you need a little patience and a variety of soft, round, light, and spiky materials. Once you've mastered the basic skills of wiring, then the fun begins. It is a good idea to wire up all the small bunches you are likely to need in advance, so that when it comes to building up the wreath you have your materials close at hand and ready to use. Speed comes with practice, but it is better to allow yourself the time to get truly creative and enjoy finding your own style.

Green zinnia

YOU WILL NEED

- **10in (25cm) flat wire wreath ring**
- **Reel of binding wire**
- **Sphagnum moss**
- **Scissors**
- **22-gauge 12in (30cm) florist's wire**
- **Green stem binding tape**
- ***Lepidium sativum*, sprayed gold**
- ***Achillea* 'White Queen'**
- **Green dyed *Ruscus aculeatus***
- **White lavender**
- **White *Gomphrena globosa***
- **Green zinnia**
- ***Gypsophila***
- ***Iris siberica* pods**
- ***Nigella* (green pod)**
- ***Eleusine***
- **White larkspur**
- **Wide cream and gold ribbon**
- **Glue gun**
- **Lichen moss**

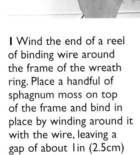

1 Wind the end of a reel of binding wire around the frame of the wreath ring. Place a handful of sphagnum moss on top of the frame and bind in place by winding around it with the wire, leaving a gap of about 1in (2.5cm) between binds.

2 Continue binding more moss to the ring, keeping it even. When you arrive back at the start, leave the reel of wire attached. Trim away any straggly moss ends.

Dyed green Ruscus aculeatus and Gypsophila

3 Wrap two 22-gauge florist's wires together with stem binding tape and bend in half to form a hanger (see pages 12–15). Position the hanger opposite the point where the binding wire is attached, and twist the ends of the wire together to mark the wreaths' top.

4 Make small, double leg bunches of material (see pages 12–15). Starting opposite the hanger, attach the bunches to the wreath by winding around the stems with the binding wire, pulling quite

tightly. Start with a bunch of gold sprayed *Lepidium sativum*, positioning it flat on the mossed wreath with the flower end pointing out of the ring. Bind around the lower part of the stems to secure the first bunch.

5 Position a bunch of the achillea flat on the wreath, to the left and a little lower than the *Lepidium*, slightly overlapping it. Secure with the wire low on the stems to help keep the arrangement flat.

6 Lay and secure a bunch of green dyed *Ruscus* to the right of and overlapping the achillea. Centrally overlapping the achillea and the *Ruscus*, attach a bunch of white lavender.

You can, of course, substitute materials used here for flowers with similar shapes. The same basic principles can be used with so many materials, colors, and styles. Try single material rings using foliage, hydrangea, marjoram, or wheat. You may want to use rustic cones and twigs, or make a therapeutic lavender and rose wreath.

A door wreath like this can be made from so many alternative plant combinations. For an elegant effect, tilt it so that the bow is at a slight angle instead of simply pointing straight downwards.

7 Continue securing bunches to the arrangement's left, right, and center by overlapping the stems. Here, bunches of white *Gomphrena* have been positioned toward the center, green zinnia on the left, *Gypsophila* on the right, *Iris siberica* pods just left of center, *Nigella* center right, followed by more gold *Lepidium* and a bunch of *Eleusine* to the right.

8 Add the bunches in random order, including some white larkspur, but remembering to look at the balance of material and color. For example, the green *Ruscus* has a very vibrant color and looks good when positioned in bunches opposite each other at even intervals around the ring. Alternating the gold *Lepidium* on the inside and outside edges at regular intervals also adds interest and pulls the arrangement together. Don't squash the bunches too closely together and ensure that the inside and outside edges of the wreath follow a fairly even line. Keep checking the balance by holding the ring up to the wall.

9 When you arrive back at the beginning, position the meeting bunches as close together as possible. Wrap the wire around the final bunch a few times then cut it.

10 Fold a length of ribbon into a large double bow and use 22-gauge wire to secure it in the middle (see pages 12–15). Position the bow at the bottom of the wreath and twist the wire ends together at the back.

Garland

Garlands can be draped on staircases, beams, mirrors, or pictures, or laid on a mantelpiece. This garland has rope and moss as its base. Change the diameter of the rope for a bulkier or more delicate finish.

    Measure your space carefully, and choose materials to lay together comfortably. This garland has a very natural design and is particularly suitable for placing over a kitchen cupboard. If you need more color, add herbs, raffia, ornamental corns, or fruits. Keep the rope flat while working and don't work too tightly. If at first you don't succeed, do try again, remembering that making garlands is not easy but tremendous fun.

YOU WILL NEED

- 48–72in (120–180cm) long, medium-thickness rope
- **Reel of binding wire**
- **Sphagnum moss**
- **Scissors**
- **22-gauge 12in (30cm) florist's wire**
- *Panicum violaceum*
- *Setaria italica*
- **Hops**
- **Wheat stalks**
- **Wheat**
- **Bearded wheat**
- **Tansy**
- **Chrysanthemum**
- **'Hen and Chickens' poppy**
- *Lepidium sativum*
- **Glue gun**
- **Stem binding tape**

1 Wind the end of a reel of binding wire around the end of the rope. Do not cut the wire. Place a handful of sphagnum moss around the rope and wind around it with the wire.

2 Continue binding moss to cover the whole rope. Wrap the wire around the other end of the rope, but do not cut the wire yet.

3 Double leg wire (pages 12–15) plenty of bunches of roughly the same thickness of *Panicum violaceum*, *Setaria italica*, hops, wheat stalks, wheat, bearded wheat, tansy, chrysanthemums, poppies, and *Lepidium sativum*. Lay all the bunches out neatly for easy access when building up the garland.

4 The *Panicum violaceum* is quite droopy, so pull a few tops out and wire together to make a neater bunch.

Setaria italica, tansy, and *Panicum violaceum*

Hops look wonderfully at home in a kitchen, draped along cupboard tops or doorways, or interweaved in a garland as shown here.

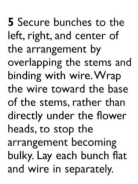

5 Secure bunches to the left, right, and center of the arrangement by overlapping the stems and binding with wire. Wrap the wire toward the base of the stems, rather than directly under the flower heads, to stop the arrangement becoming bulky. Lay each bunch flat and wire in separately.

6 Continue binding bunches, keeping the hops, poppies, and chrysanthemum in the center and the wheats and lepidium at the edges. Try to follow a repeating pattern. Place the rope against a wall regularly to make sure it sits flat and

that the materials are evenly distributed throughout. Replace material if necessary.

7 Bind as far as you can. Secure a few bunches facing in the opposite direction at the end, to finish the rope.

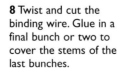

8 Twist and cut the binding wire. Glue in a final bunch or two to cover the stems of the last bunches.

9 Gutter two 22-gauge florist's wires together and bend in half to form a hanger (see pages 12–15). Make a second hanger and attach one to each end of the rope, at the back.

Wired rustic arch

An arch can be used in many locations around the home, such as on a beam, above a doorway or window, or over a picture or mirror. A rustic arch like this can easily be transformed with the use of a sumptuous ribbon instead of the more subtle, thick burlap.

Small bunches of material, including cedar roses that are gathered in the fall or winter, and twigs are tied with garden twine and arranged along a cane arch. There are, of course, any number of combinations of materials that could be used; simply master the basic skills of wiring and away you go.

Cedar rose and sponge mushroom

YOU WILL NEED

- **22-gauge 12in (30cm) florist's wire**
- **Scissors**
- **Oak leaves, sprayed basil green**
- **White larkspur**
- **Terracotta achillea**
- **Cream *Celosia***
- **'Mini' poppy, sprayed basil green**
- ***Sorghum nigrum***
- **Peach dyed broom bloom**
- **Orange *Gomphrena globosa***
- **Cedar roses**
- **Twigs**
- **Garden twine**
- **Glue gun**
- **Sponge mushroom**
- **Green coco moss**
- **Reel of binding wire**
- **Cane arch**
- **Reel of burlap**
- **Stem binding tape**

Celosia and Sorghum nigrum

1 Double leg wire small bunches of oak leaves, white larkspur, terracotta achillea, cream *Celosia*, poppy, *Sorghum nigrum*, peach broom bloom, and orange *Gomphrena* (see pages 12–15). The bunches of long material should be about 4–5in (10–13cm) long, the bunches of rounder heads about 3in (7.5cm) long.

2 Wire up four to six cedar roses like cones (see pages 12–15). Cut twigs into 6in (15cm) lengths. Bundle five to six twigs together with wire and tie over with garden twine. Make two twig bunches. Glue a double leg wire to each sponge mushroom piece. Tease out handfuls of green coco moss and wire up into double leg bunches.

3 Keep the bunches in separate piles to choose from when you build up the arch. Make up more bunches than you think you will need.

4 Thread the end of a reel of binding wire through the end of the arch and twist to secure. Lay an oak leaf bunch flat on the arch and wrap the binding wire around the stems.

5 Take a reel of burlap and form into a loop. Place the loop on top of the oak stems and wrap.

6 Secure bunches to the left, right, and center of the arrangement by overlapping the stems and binding with wire. Remember to balance the colors on alternate sides. Lay each bunch flat and wire in separately. Remember that the display needs to sit flat against the wall, so keep all the wires on top of the arch where they will be covered up.

7 Work the burlap down the arch as you go and bring it out as a loop at regular intervals.

The wiring up of bunches requires a certain degree of patience. Make up more bunches than you think you will need, so that you don't have to stop part of the way through the design process to make more.

This rustic arch is a vibrant yet graceful design for the home. The traditional meaning of its various parts add credence to its appeal: Gomphrena is linked to immortality, larkspur to capriciousness.

10 Position the cedar roses and mushrooms before gluing them in.

8 Continue adding bunches and bringing in burlap loops. Place the arch against a wall regularly to make sure it sits flat so that the materials are evenly distributed throughout. Remember the sides need to fill out as well as the front. Replace material if necessary.

9 When you get to the end, wrap the wire around the final bunch a few times, thread it through the back of the arch and cut. Glue a few bunches on at the end, facing in the opposite direction, to cover the last stems and round off the arch.

11 Glue in the two twig bunches roughly centrally and at different angles.

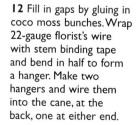

12 Fill in gaps by gluing in coco moss bunches. Wrap 22-gauge florist's wire with stem binding tape and bend in half to form a hanger. Make two hangers and wire them into the cane, at the back, one at either end.

Cone drop

A sculptural drop constructed with cones is a labor of love, but it really lasts. The preparation—seemingly endless wiring and guttering—is particularly time-consuming, but such attention to detail is well worth the effort. Prepare all the materials in advance, then put aside plenty of time to enjoy the challenge of building up a demanding and intricate design.

To master the basic skills, think of the overall shape and start with small items, moving on to medium, then large, with the addition of wheat growing from single ears to groups of five. Have confidence and everything will come together.

Remember the secrets you have learned, and enjoy the wealth of brown tones and textures provided by nature in abundance. Don't be too methodical in your approach, and this original design will be preserved in time.

100

YOU WILL NEED

- 22-gauge 12in (30cm) florist's wire
- Stem binding tape
- Scissors
- Wheat
- Various sizes of poppy heads
- Baby lotus
- Cypress
- Wellingtonia cones
- Pine cones
- Alder cones
- Brown *Ruscus aculeatus*
- *Iris siberica*
- Cedar cones
- Hackea
- Liquidambar
- Sponge mushrooms
- *Sisyrinchium* seed heads
- Natural oak leaves
- Cedar roses
- Beechmasts
- Baby larch cones
- 2 garden canes
- 2 18-gauge 12in (30cm) florist's wires
- Glue gun
- Binding wire
- Cream and gold hessian ribbon

Hackea

Liquidambar

Cedar rose

Beechmast

Pine cone

Wellingtonia cone

1 Individually wire and gutter (see pages 12–15) stems of wheat, poppy (big pod), baby lotus, cypress, wellingtonia cones, pine cones, alder cones, cedar cones, brown *Ruscus aculeatus*, *Iris siberica*, hackea, liquidambar, sponge mushrooms, *Sisyrinchium* seed heads, natural oak leaves, cedar roses, beechmasts, and baby larch cones.

3 Wrap two 18-gauge wires with stem bending tape and bend in half to make a strong hook. Glue the hook to one end of the cane and secure further with binding wire.

2 Bind two garden canes together with stem binding tape, to make one thick cane.

4 Wrap some stem binding tape around the bottom of the cane. Do not cut the tape. Start by adding tall, pointed material, such as wheat, and wrap around the guttered wire with the tape.

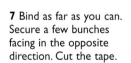

5 Secure material to the left, right, and center of the arrangement by overlapping the stems and binding with tape. Start with the smallest materials and build up to heavier pieces.

6 Gradually bring in larger materials, remembering to build up the sides as well as the center. The materials do not follow a regular pattern, but do try to make sure they are fairly evenly distributed throughout. Place the cane against a wall regularly to judge its balance and replace material if necessary.

7 Bind as far as you can. Secure a few bunches facing in the opposite direction. Cut the tape.

8 Make a double bow and glue it in. Glue in a final cone or two to neaten.

When the cedar tree sheds its cones, the cones shatter on impact with the ground, leaving cedar roses that have the appearance of wooden flowers. These are perfect for imparting rough-hewn texture and warmth to a dried flower design.

Wedding favor

Wedding favors can be made to give to the bride, or as presents for wedding guests. This favor features a lucky horseshoe as a present for the bride, but equally you could decorate a traditional wooden spoon, or even a rolling pin. For the guests, you could make a tiny nosegay of flowers, perhaps a silvery decorated bell, or a wonderful lace bag filled with a pot pourri of petals.

Horseshoes make an enchanting keepsake.

YOU WILL NEED

- **18-gauge 12in (30cm) florist's wire**
- **Stem binding tape**
- **Scissors**
- **Horseshoe**
- **Silver rose wire**
- ***Artemesia ludoviciana* 'Silver Queen'**
- **'Mini' poppy**
- **Lavender *Gomphrena globosa***
- **Cerise *Gomphrena globosa***
- **Purple zinnia**
- ***Achillea millefolium* 'Summer Pastels'**
- ***Echinops***
- **Glue gun**
- **Natural reindeer moss**
- **Artificial sparkly turquoise berries**
- **Thin, pale blue voile ribbon**
- **Thin, silver voile ribbon**

1 Join two pairs of 18-gauge wires together by wrapping them with stem binding tape. Mold the guttered wires around a horseshoe to give a horseshoe shape.

3 Wrap some stem binding tape around one end of the wire horseshoe and leave attached. Position the first bunch on the wire and wrap around the stems with the tape. Start to secure the material to the left, right, and center of the ring by overlapping the stems and binding with tape.

5 Glue natural reindeer moss to the back of the horseshoe to tidy the edges, and glue a few sparkly turquoise berries to the display's front.

6 Fold two lengths of pale blue ribbon into double bows and use silver wire to secure them in the middle (see pages 12–15). Attach the silver voile ribbon to either end of the horseshoe, and glue the ribbons at either end.

2 Use silver rose wire to wire small mixed bunches using all or some of the material (see pages 12–15).

Silver voile ribbon, lavender *Gomphrena globosa*, and cerise *Gomphrena globosa*

4 Keep adding bunches until you reach the other end.

Wedding corsage

Wedding corsages are fun to make, and if you have time, why not make a corsage or buttonhole for each guest, perhaps to be handed out from a garlanded traditional basket, for a delightful keepsake.

You can also prepare your own confetti with garden petals, and tie them in a pretty bag to give out to guests to strew over the happy couple. Wedding color schemes change with the seasons, but dried flower materials in all colors are always available.

A lady's corsage to be worn by the mother of the bride, or to adorn a wedding gift.

YOU WILL NEED

- **Silver rose wire**
- **Scissors**
- **_Artemesia ludoviciana_ 'Silver Queen'**
- **'Mini' poppy**
- **Lavender _Gomphrena globosa_**
- **Cerise _Gomphrena globosa_**
- **Purple zinnia**
- **_Achillea millefolium_ 'Summer Pastels'**
- **_Echinops_**
- **Artificial sparkly turquoise berries**
- **Stem binding tape**
- **Thin, silver voile ribbon**
- **Silver cord**

1 Use silver rose wire to individually wire (see pages 12–15) stems of artemesia, poppy, lavender and cerise _Gomphrena_, purple zinnia, achillea, _Echinops_, and artificial sparkly turquoise berries.

2 Gutter all the wires (see pages 12–15).

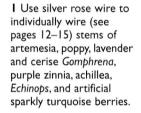

3 Hold the first pieces of material in one hand and wrap around the guttered stems with stem binding tape to join.

Use the same, but fewer, materials, bound around a guttered 22-gauge florist's wire with silver cord, to make a buttonhole. Use the larger heads for a more masculine look.

4 Add more material and wind the tape around the stems as you go.

5 Decide where to finish and leave the long guttered wires and tape attached for now.

6 Fold a length of ribbon into a small double bow and use silver cord to secure it in the middle (see pages 12–15). Tie the cord around the back of the guttered wires.

7 Trim the guttered wires, leaving enough stem to hold the corsage with. Fold the tape lengthwise over the stems to cover them. Wrap the tape around the stem beneath the flowers and cut.

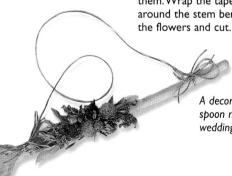

A decorated wooden spoon makes a fun wedding shower gift.

Wedding headdress

The year-round availability of dried flowers makes the bride's choice of wedding colors very easy to follow. For headdresses, you can design hair bands, circles, clips, or single flower pins to be woven into the hair. Delicate flowers are easily wired up and bound on.

Silver cord

Gomphrena globosa is a wonderfully versatile plant, and is available in a wide variety of tones including white, lavender, cerise, orange, and red. It is ideal for intricate work and well worth the trouble of growing in one's own garden.

CELEBRATIONS

YOU WILL NEED

- **Tape measure**
- **22-gauge 12in (30cm) florist's wire**
- **Scissors**
- **Stem binding tape**
- **Silver rose wire**
- *Artemesia ludoviciana* **'Silver Queen'**
- **'Mini' poppy**
- **Lavender** *Gomphrena globosa*
- **Cerise** *Gomphrena globosa*
- **Purple zinnia**
- *Achillea millefolium* **'Summer Pastels'**
- *Echinops*
- **Artificial sparkly turquoise berries**
- **Thin, silver gauze ribbon**
- **Silver cord**

1 Measure the head that will wear the headdress. Join pairs of 22-gauge wires together by wrapping them with stem binding tape to meet the length needed.

2 Bend the guttered wires into a circle. Loop one end and gutter over the join to make an eye. Loop the other end but do not gutter the join, to make the hook.

Wired and guttered *Echinops* **and 'Mini' poppy**

3 Use silver rose wire to individually wire (see pages 12–15) stems of artemesia, poppy, lavender and cerise *Gomphrena*, purple zinnia, achillea, *Echinops*, and artificial sparkly turquoise berries.

4 Gutter all the wires (see pages 12–15).

5 Wrap some stem binding tape around one end of the ring and leave attached. Position the first material on the ring and wrap around the stems with the tape. Start to secure the material to the left, right, and center of the ring by overlapping the stems and binding with tape. Keep all the wires on top of the ring.

With the exception of a few herbaceous species, artemisias are grown for their silver-gray, feathery, aromatic foliage. Here, Artemisa ludoviciana 'Silver Queen' blends in beautifully with the silver of the headdress.

6 Keep adding material until you reach the other end. Stand back from your work regularly to make sure the materials are evenly distributed throughout. Remember the sides need to fill out as well as the front.

7 Fold a length of ribbon into a large double bow with long tails (see pages 12–15). Use silver cord to secure the bow in the middle, leaving long ends.

8 Join the headdress together with the hook and eye. Use the silver cord to tie the bow over the hook and eye to disguise the join. Leave a trail of ribbon to hang down, but not so much so that it annoys the wearer.

Wedding bouquet

For weddings, wonderful effects can be obtained with dried flowers. The choice here is a compact, pretty bouquet in a soft combination of colors that are feminine but not frilly.

Dried flower wedding arrangements can be made up well in advance. I have spent many happy hours with brides, designing the wedding bouquets of their dreams. The choice for bouquets is endless: they may be wired, tied, or, as here, formed on a holder. Make them flowing, arched, or formed in the shape of a simple posy.

Cerise *Gomphrena globosa* and lavender *Gomphrena globosa*

YOU WILL NEED

- **Eucalyptus**
- **22-gauge 12in (30cm) florist's wire**
- **Small foam bouquet holder**
- **Glue gun**
- **Scissors**
- ***Achillea millefolium* 'Summer Pastels'**
- **Purple zinnia**
- **Silver rose wire**
- **Lavender *Gomphrena globosa***
- **Cerise *Gomphrena globosa***
- ***Echinops***
- **'Mini' poppy**
- ***Artemesia ludoviciana* 'Silver Queen'**
- **Artificial sparkly turquoise berries**
- **Wide, silver-blue voile ribbon**
- **Silver cord**
- **Thin, silver voile ribbon**

1 Thread 22-gauge wire behind the vein of a eucalyptus leaf (see pages 12–15). You will need about ten leaves.

2 Insert the leaves into the foam at the base of the bouquet holder and glue for extra security.

Silver-blue voile ribbon

3 Wire small bunches of achillea stems, and five or six individual stems of purple zinnia (see pages 12–15). Use silver rose wire to wire the more delicate lavender and cerise *Gomphrena*.

4 Push the wired materials into the foam ball and glue for added stability. Start with achillea bunches just above the eucalyptus leaves.

5 Insert individual stems of *Echinops* in a circle above the achillea.

6 Push in a circle of zinnia, above the *Echinops*.

7 Add about three lavender *Gomphrena* heads to fill the center circle of the arrangement.

Dried wedding displays can be lavish, incorporating a profusion of roses and peonies, or relatively simple with just grasses and herbs. Brown and cream tones can be created with cones and fungi, or a medieval theme enhanced by purple artichokes and red pomegranates.

8 Add alternate heads of lavender and cerise *Gomphrena* under the *Echinops*.

9 Insert poppy above the cerise *Gomphrena* between the *Echinops*.

10 Glue artemesia leaves between each *Gomphrena* above the achillea.

Dried flower wedding bouquets are the perfect memento of a special day. Here the sparkling turquoise berries pick up the color of the Echinops and the ribbon, and similar tones in the bridesmaids' dresses.

11 Pull a few stems of turquoise berries away from the main stem and glue one in the center of the bouquet and others between the zinnia.

12 Fold a length of wide silver-blue voile ribbon into a large double bow and secure in the center with silver cord (see pages 12–15). With thin voile silver ribbon, make a bow with three loops and secure with silver cord.

13 Wrap a length of silver-blue ribbon lengthwise over the bouquet holder handle. Wrap the end of the ribbon around the handle and glue in place at the top of the stalk under the bouquet.

14 Look at the bouquet in a mirror and decide on the front. Position the bows over the handle at the front and tie in place at the back with the silver cord.

Easter basket

Easter is a fun time to make things, to involve children, or remember friends with a special homemade gift. Baskets are natural companions to Easter, giving a true country feel and a hint of nostalgia. This basket is designed to display free-range eggs, delicious Easter cookies, homemade simnel cake, or perhaps Easter eggs. It's the thought that counts, but presentation makes a gift just that extra bit special.

An egg cup is trimmed with reindeer moss, cream Santolina, and yellow raffia.

YOU WILL NEED

- **Flat basket with a handle**
- **Glue gun**
- **Sphagnum moss**
- **Twigs**
- **Garden twine**
- **Scissors**
- **Ornamental eggs**
- **Palm**
- *Lepidium sativum*
- **Cream *Santolina***
- **Yellow achillea**
- *Phlomis fruticosa*
- **Willow in bud**
- **White feathers**
- **Wide, yellow gingham ribbon**
- **Large raw egg**
- **Diluted bleach**
- **Yellow reindeer moss**
- **Straw**

Straw, willow, and an egg

1 Glue sphagnum moss all around the rim of a flat basket, taking the moss a little way up the handles.

2 Take a generous handful of moss and form it into a bird's nest shape. Add a few twigs randomly sticking out and wrap garden twine all around the nest to bind the materials securely.

3 Nestle the nest into the basket, close to the edge, underneath one side of the handle. Glue in place and add a few eggs.

A small rush basket is filled with reindeer moss, Solidago, willow, and heads of Phlomis fruticosa for a touch of springtime.

4 In one hand, form an open bunch using palm at the back, *Lepidium sativum*, also at the back, and cream *Santolina*, yellow achillea, *Phlomis fruticosa*, and willow staggered in front. Add in three white feathers and tie the bunch with twine. Make a second bunch in the same way.

The design described here is simple and inexpensive. You can experiment with your own ideas, adapting the rules to your own specification. You could use feathers and straw, willow, yellow ribbon, egg shells, and moss for example.

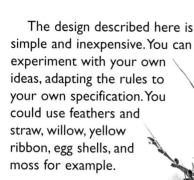

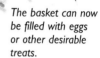

5 Glue one bunch very firmly to the mossed rim to the left of the nest of eggs, so that the flowers point out of the basket and toward the handle. This will be the front of the display. Tie with the twine to double secure.

7 Fold a length of ribbon into a double bow (see pages 12–15). Make two bows.

The basket can now be filled with eggs or other desirable treats.

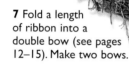

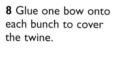

8 Glue one bow onto each bunch to cover the twine.

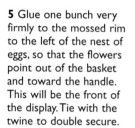

6 Glue the second bunch to the handle by the nest, so that the flowers climb up the handle and are seen from the front. Secure with twine.

9 Crack open the raw egg. Wash the shells with diluted bleach then glue the two halves under the handle opposite the nest. Fill with reindeer moss.

10 Cover the base of the basket with a layer of straw.

Thanksgiving sign

This rustic Thanksgiving sign evokes the spirit of harvest, and is designed to hang on a door as a welcome sign to family and friends gathering for the Thanksgiving vacation.

    After binding together raspberry canes to construct a strong base to work on, each sign can be personalized to signify the importance of one's home. Try to depict your family, what you grow, your home, and what Thanksgiving means to you, then trim it up with the gifts of nature.

Dark and light green reindeer moss, beechmasts, and cob nuts

C E L E B R A T I O N S

YOU WILL NEED
- **Raspberry canes**
- **Secateurs**
- **Garden twine**
- **Scissors**
- **Dry florist's foam**
- **Knife**
- **Glue gun**
- **Binding wire**
- **Dark green reindeer moss**
- **Light green reindeer moss**
- **Wheat**
- **Tiny basket**
- **Chili peppers**
- **1 small** *Zea mays* **strawberry corncob**

- **Apple slices**
- **Blood orange slices**
- **Red beans**
- **Split lentils**
- **6 pebbles**
- **22-gauge 12in (30cm) florist's wire**
- **Raffia**
- **Miniature garden fork**
- **Beechmasts**
- **Cob nuts**
- **Dark green dyed** *Ruscus aculeatus*
- **Larch cones**
- **Yellow achillea**
- **Red dyed oak leaves**
- **2 gingerbread figures**
- **Gingerbread heart**
- **Plaited hessian rope**

1 Cut ten 24in (60cm) lengths of raspberry cane and five 6in (15cm) lengths. Use garden twine to bind two groups of five long canes together. Lay the two groups parallel to each other.

2 Lay the five shorter canes as struts across the two long edges, evenly spaced apart. The struts should protrude slightly over the edge of the long canes. Criss-cross garden twine over the canes to bind the struts and edges together.

3 Cut a block of dry florist's foam in half lengthwise. Cut this half in half and halve again.

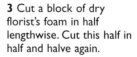

4 Glue the two thin slices of foam firmly onto the cane base. Anchor with binding wire.

5 Glue a thin, flat layer of dark green reindeer moss over the foam.

6 Glue a thin layer of light green reindeer moss to form an edge around the sides.

A raspberry cane and some wheat heads

Have fun writing the words "welcome" or "home sweet home" as an alternative to this pictorial Thanksgiving sign.

10 Glue the half basket to the moss toward the right edge of the sign.

11 Fill the basket by gluing in a few wheat heads, chili peppers, a small strawberry corncob, and apple and blood orange slices. Glue a few red beans and split lentils on either side of the basket.

7 Cut about eight small pieces of raspberry cane and form ito the shape of a naive house. Glue to the moss, just left of center.

8 Glue wheat stalks into the roof shape to look like thatch.

12 Form a garden path by gluing a few pebbles along the bottom of the sign.

9 Cut off the handle of a tiny basket and then cut the basket in half lengthwise.

13 Wire a bunch of six wheat heads, wrapping the wire around the middle of the stems and keeping the wire ends at right angles to the bunch (see pages 12–15). Insert the wire into the foam and glue in place.

14 Glue a small raffia bow to cover the wire on the wheat bunch and cross the bow with a glued on miniature garden fork.

15 Glue alternate beechmasts and cob nuts in a line along the bottom, and dark green *Ruscus* and larch cones in the top corners.

16 Glue yellow achillea between the split lentils and the house, and red oak leaves above to look like a tree. Glue two gingerbread figures to the left of the house, on the path, and a gingerbread heart on the house.

17 Tie one end of some plaited hessian rope around the top rung of the sign's frame, and the other end on the other side, to form a hanger.

Thanksgiving table center

This cornucopia display uses plants that capture the wonderful colors of harvest, such as sunflowers and ornamental corns—red, strawberry, and the colorful Harlequin—that all evoke a feeling of abundance. The corn husks also make ideal bows, natural in color and style, while groups of natural wheat keep their color beautifully.

　　The cornucopia baskets have been put together to enable us to create an all-around centerpiece. Add candlesticks, make napkin rings from corn husks, or set a name card in a wheat bunch, before you weigh the table down with turkey, sweet potato, and pumpkin pie.

YOU WILL NEED

- **2 cornucopia baskets**
- **Binding wire**
- **Scissors**
- **Dry florist's foam**
- **Knife**
- **Sphagnum moss**
- **22-gauge 12in (30cm) florist's wire**
- **Wheat**
- **2 sunflowers**
- ***Zea mays* corn husks**
- ***Zea mays* corncobs, (red, strawberry, and 'Harlequin')**
- ***Sorghum nigrum***
- **Poppy (big pod)**

1 Position two cornucopia baskets, cone ends overlapping slightly, and thread binding wire through the weaving of both baskets to join them.

2 Cut dry florist's foam blocks to fit inside the baskets and stand proud of each rim by about 1in (2.5cm). Push the foam into each basket and wedge in place by packing sphagnum moss around the sides.

3 Lightly cover the foam with moss and pin in place (see pages 12–15).

4 Treat each basket in roughly the same way, pushing the same materials into the foam. Start by wiring six bunches of nine to eleven wheat stems (see pages 12–15) and arranging three bunches in each foam block, around the edge.

Red *Zea mays* corncob and *Zea mays* 'Harlequin' corncob

5 Push a sunflower stem between the top of each basket and the foam, so that the flower is the centerpiece.

After the festivities are over, separate the cornucopia baskets to rest them on kitchen cupboards or to use as an unusual wall feature.

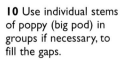

113

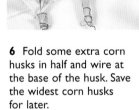

6 Fold some extra corn husks in half and wire at the base of the husk. Save the widest corn husks for later.

8 Push the wired corns and husks into the foam at various angles, keeping an eye on color balance.

11 Fold four of the widest corn husks in half and wire at the base to form the basis of a bow. Keep four more wide husks to form the tails. Wrap the wire of the husk loops around the husk tails to make two bows, and wire one to the edge of each basket.

9 Insert individual stems of *Sorghum nigrum* close to the wheat bunches.

10 Use individual stems of poppy (big pod) in groups if necessary, to fill the gaps.

7 Wire ten corncobs of a mixture of colors (see pages 12–15).

***Sorghum nigrum* and sunflower**

Black moss

Halloween hat

Chinese lantern

Why not try this simple idea for a halloween party table? A witch's hat of any size can be transformed with some verve and imagination. Look around you for colorfully wrapped sweets to pin on for a trick-or-treat hat, or extend your repertoire to food with edible goodies speared on cocktail sticks for a colorful centerpiece.

Nigella orientalis, srayed black

Black moss provides a wonderful dramatic contrast to the bright orange of the Chinese lanterns, while *Nigella orientalis* adds a spooky dimension, especially when sprayed black.

CELEBRATIONS

YOU WILL NEED

- **Fresh pumpkin**
- **Knife**
- **Glue gun**
- **Black moss**
- **Dry florist's foam cone**
- **Garden twine**
- **Scissors**
- **22-gauge 12in (30cm) florist's wire**
- **Chinese lanterns**
- ***Nigella orientalis,* sprayed black**
- **Birch twigs, sprayed black**
- **Binding wire**
- **Black cartridge paper**
- **Novelty spider's web**

1 Cut off the top of a fresh pumpkin and hollow out the insides.

2 Glue black moss all over a dry florist's foam cone so that the black side of the moss is visible.

3 Wrap an even spiral of garden twine around the mossed cone as a guideline for positioning the next material. Use 22-gauge florist's wire pins to fix the twine in place (see pages 12–15).

4 Pull off individual Chinese lanterns from the main stem, leaving a small stalk attached on each. Gently bend back the petals to open the flowers.

5 Glue a line of Chinese lanterns onto the spiral of garden twine, positioning the flowers close together so that the twine can not be seen.

Broomsticks are a must and quick to construct. Make various sizes to hang from the ceiling or lie against the corner of a room. Cobwebs can also be easily constructed with a homemade wire frame and some thread.

This theatrical design is a delightful alternative to more typical Halloween creations. The Chinese lanterns can be peeled open to reveal their central orange-red berries, as shown here.

8 Cut a circle of black cartridge paper wider than the base of the hollowed-out pumpkin. Place the pumpkin on the paper. Put the cone hat in the pumpkin. Finish with the twig broomstick and a novelty spider's web.

7 Gather a handful of thin birch twigs and bunch them around a thicker twig to look like a witch's broomstick. Wrap binding wire around the twigs to secure.

6 Push short stems of black *Nigella orientalis* into the foam in a spiral on top of the Chinese lantern coil.

Bright red rose heads and broom bloom

Christmas nut basket

Green dyed oak leaves and green reindeer moss

Decorated baskets for nuts, homemade sweets, cutlery, Christmas fruits, hampers, cookies, or warm mince pies can make your table or gifts just a little more welcoming during the holiday season, adding finishing touches to the home at a very special time of the year. For this Christmas nut basket we have chosen a festive color scheme of red, green, and gold, with complementary ribbons.

Baskets can also be given a whole new look with a glimmer of gold spray paint. Remember though that the color of gold varies considerably, so test the spray before you commit yourself to it.

CELEBRATIONS

YOU WILL NEED

- **Shallow basket**
- **Glue gun**
- **Green dyed oak leaves**
- **Green reindeer moss**
- **Wellingtonia cones, sprayed gold**
- **Tiny lotus heads**
- **Cinnamon sticks**
- **Poppy, sprayed gold**
- **Orange slices**
- **Gold cord**
- **Scissors**
- **Red broom bloom**
- **Beechmasts**
- **Acorns**
- **Alder cones**
- **Red roses**
- **Wide, red and gold tartan ribbon**

2 Individually glue the materials over the moss, starting with the largest items. Glue a pair of gold wellingtonia cones centrally, with a natural lotus head in between. Add in a pair of cinnamon sticks adjacent to the left cone. Glue a pair of gold poppies toward the left edge. Bring in a couple of orange slices nestled against the cones.

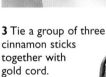

3 Tie a group of three cinnamon sticks together with gold cord.

4 Glue the cinnamon stick bundle under the handle on the right. Glue in small pieces of red broom bloom. Use beechmasts, acorns, and a little moss to fill in gaps. Add in groups of tiny alder cones that stand slightly proud.

5 Glue in a few red roses to add color.

6 Fold a length of ribbon into a large double bow (see pages 12–15). Glue the bow in by the right handle. Glue a couple of ribbon tails on the left and right edges to complete.

1 Glue a few green oak leaves and some reindeer moss on one rim of a shallow basket, from one corner almost along the full length.

The decorated shallow basket is brimming over with nuts, ready to welcome guests.

Acorn cups, alder cones, and a gold sprayed walnut shell

Table ideas

The festive table is the centerpiece of the holiday season, so have fun making individual place settings. A walnut transforms into a candle base, as could an oyster shell or small flower pot.

It is easy to design an elegant name card to make your guests feel special, or to buy extra ribbon when decorating the tree or table wreath to form into napkin rings. Alternatively, raffia and cones or fruit create a natural look.

SAFETY
✿ Never leave a candle burning unattended, or let the candle burn down so low that the flame licks the dried flower material.

YOU WILL NEED

- **Glue gun**
- **Scissors**
- **Gold thread**

To make various table arrangements you can use some or all of the materials listed:

- **Dry florist's foam**
- **Knife**
- **22-gauge 12in (30cm) florist's wire**
- **Green reindeer moss**
- **Small green dyed oak leaves**
- **Alder cones, sprayed gold**
- **Acorn cups**
- **Bright red rose**
- **Decorative card**
- **Wide, tartan voile ribbon**
- **Small gold candles**
- **Gold cord**
- **Old walnut**
- **Gilt cream**
- **Reinforced nylon plaster**

Name card

1 Cut a slot into a small block of dry florist's foam, to hold the name card.

2 Pin green reindeer moss over the foam (see pages 12–15).

3 In front of the groove in the foam, glue an arrangement of green oak leaves, gold alder cones, acorn cups, a bright red rose, and gold thread.

4 Write the person's name on a piece of pretty card and slot it into the groove.

Napkin ring

1 Glue the ends of a short length of tartan ribbon together to create the ring.

2 Glue an arrangement of green oak leaves, green reindeer moss, gold alder cones, acorn cups, a bright red rose, and fine gold cord over the ribbon join.

Candle bunch

1 Tie together three small gold candles with gold cord.

2 Push a few green oak leaves between the candles and the cord, and glue an arrangement to the leaves, not the candle, using a bright red rose, green reindeer moss, an acorn cup, gold alder cones, and gold thread.

Candle display

1 Break an old walnut in half—an old nut is easier to break.

2 Rub the half shell with gilt cream (see pages 12–15).

3 Push some reinforced nylon plaster into the shell and push a small gold candle into the clay.

4 Glue an arrangement onto the plaster around the candle, taking care not to use heavy materials in a position that will topple the candle over, using green oak leaves, acorn cups, gold alder cones, a bright red rose, and gold thread.

Gift wrap

There is a huge feeling of accomplishment to designing and making your own Christmas decorations and wrappings. A beautifully decorated tree, piles of carefully wrapped presents, twinkling lights, and the scent of fresh pine conjure up the comforting traditional image of a homemade festive season.

When wrapping gifts, choose your paper carefully from the wealth of designs available. The simplest of presents can be transformed with a little effort at the wrapping stage.

CELEBRATIONS

YOU WILL NEED

- **Glue gun**
- **Scissors**

To decorate various gifts you can use some or all of the materials listed:

- **Handmade papers**
- **Gold cord**
- **Bright red rose**
- **Larch cones, sprayed gold**
- **Garden twine, sprayed gold**
- **Old walnut**
- **Gilt cream**
- **Small green oak leaves**
- **Red broom bloom**
- **Red *Celosia***
- **Green reindeer moss**
- **Artificial red berries**
- **'Hen and Chickens' poppy**
- **Brown paper**
- **Orange slice**

This parcel, wrapped in brown paper and red and gold ribbon, has been embellished with a simple glued, central arrangement using green oak leaves, red broom bloom, and an orange slice and a cinnamon stick.

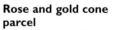

Rose and gold cone parcel

I Wrap a parcel in green and gold handmade paper and gold cord.

2 Pull off a few petals from a bright red rose.

3 Glue rose petals and leaves and gold larch cones in a staggered line following the line of gold cord.

A wine bottle wrapped in brown paper has had an arrangement using a gold woven ring, gold wheat, and gold garden twine glued on close to the neck.

Red and gold ribbon

Walnut parcel

I Wrap a parcel in green handmade paper and gold garden twine.

2 Break an old walnut in half and rub with gilt cream (see pages 12–15).

3 Glue an arrangement of green oak leaves, red broom bloom, red *Celosia*, green reindeer moss, and an artificial red berry inside the shell.

Flower parcel

I Glue the frill of a gold 'Hen and Chickens' poppy on a parcel wrapped with brown paper and gold cord. Glue an orange slice quarter on top as the flower head.

2 Add some green reindeer moss at the base of the flower. Cut the center of the poppy open to cut out the flower's leaves and stem, and glue to the parcel.

Artificial red berries

Christmas decorations

Carrying through the traditional Christmas color scheme of red, green, and gold, look around you for inspirational material to make ornaments to dress your tree. Choose a variety of textures and materials with a Christmas feel: pine cones, walnuts, and cinnamon sticks spring to mind. Popcorn, candy, and fruit slices are also effective if brought together in a theme.

A tiny terracotta pot has been rubbed with gilt cream (see pages 12–15) and filled with a little dry florist's foam. Glued onto the foam are three artificial red berries, a gold lotus seed head, a small green oak leaf, some green reindeer moss, and gold cord formed into bows.

YOU WILL NEED

- **Glue gun**
- **Scissors**
- **Gold cord**

A tiny wicker ring has been rubbed with gilt cream. Glued to one side are small green oak leaves, acorn cups, gold alder cones, an artificial red berry, some green reindeer moss, a tartan bow, and some gold cord.

To make various Christmas decorations you can use some or all of the materials listed:

- **Cinnamon sticks**
- **Beechmasts**
- **Alder cones, natural and sprayed gold**
- **Artificial red berries**
- **Green reindeer moss**
- **Tartan ribbon**
- **Tiny terracotta pots**
- **Gilt cream**
- **Dry florist's foam**
- **Lotus seed head, sprayed gold**
- **Small green dyed oak leaves**
- **Dried lychee**

- **Acorn cups**
- **Red broom bloom**
- **Tiny wicker ring**
- **Zea strawberry corn**
- **Gold florist's spray paint**
- **Tiny woven basket, sprayed gold**
- **Poppy pod, sprayed gold**
- **Walnut**
- **Wheat, sprayed gold**
- **Raffia**
- **Red rose petals**
- **Cone, sprayed gold**

Ten gold wheat stems have been tied together with gold cord and a raffia bow. Two artificial red berries have simply been glued onto the wheat just above the bow.

A dried lychee has been rubbed with gilt cream. Glued on top is an acorn cup, three natural alder cones, some red broom bloom, a tartan bow, some gold thread, moss, and a berry.

Four cinnamon sticks are tied together with gold cord. Glued onto the arrangement is a beechmast, a gold alder cone, two natural alder cones, two artificial red berries, green reindeer moss, and a tartan bow.

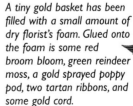

A tiny gold basket has been filled with a small amount of dry florist's foam. Glued onto the foam is some red broom bloom, green reindeer moss, a gold sprayed poppy pod, two tartan ribbons, and some gold cord.

The husk of a Zea mays strawberry corn has been painted with gold spray paint. Three artificial red berries, three acorn cups, green reindeer moss, and some gold cord have been glued in place around the base of the husk.

Christmas wreath

Welcome Christmas guests into your home with this heart-warming wreath. If you are trimming your eucalyptus tree, make up the basic ring with fresh foliage bunches, and harvest materials for gilding: enjoy foraging for cones and other gifts of nature. A little planning leaves you more time to enjoy your preparations later.

Do remember that Christmas is the one time of year when we can gild and sparkle to our heart's content, so have fun choosing from the wide array of spray cans of glitter that are available to buy.

CELEBRATIONS

YOU WILL NEED

- 10in (25cm) flat wire wreath ring
- Reel of binding wire
- Sphagnum moss
- Scissors
- 22-gauge 12in (30cm) florist's wire
- Eucalyptus
- Newspaper
- Dark green florist's spray paint
- Gold florist's spray paint
- 3 gold lotus
- 3 gold holfords cones
- 3 gold cedar cones
- Gold ting ting
- Red glitter wheat
- Red glitter birch
- Red broom bloom
- Artificial red berries
- Orange slices
- Wide, red and gold voile ribbon
- Stem binding tape

1 Wind the end of a reel of binding wire around the frame of a wreath ring. Place a handful of sphagnum moss on top of the frame and bind in place by winding around it with the wire, leaving a gap of about 1in (2.5cm) between binds. Cover the whole ring with moss.

2 Wire together thick bunches of eucalyptus (see pages 12–15). You will need about 18 to 20 bunches.

3 Attach the eucalyptus bunches to the left, right, and center of the wreath by winding around the stems with binding wire, pulling quite tightly. Bind around the lower part of the stems and keep all the wires on top of the wreath so that it will sit flat on a wall.

4 Cover your work surface with newspaper and spray the eucalyptus wreath dark green with gold highlights, following the paint manufacturer's instructions.

Gold ting ting, red glitter birch, and red glitter wheat

This wreath looks stunning in any setting, and carries with it memories of warm summer and fall days spent collecting goodies.

Golden lotus heads add dramatic substance to a design, especially when nestled in amongst cones.

5 Lay out three arrangements, equally spaced around the wreath, using a gold lotus, gold holfords cone, gold cedar cone, gold ting ting, and wired bunches (see pages 12–15) of three to four stems of red glitter wheat, three to four stems of red glitter birch, about eight stems of red broom bloom, four of artificial berries, and wired pairs of orange slices (see pages 12–15). Make sure the arrangements point in the same direction, then glue them in place.

6 Fold a length of ribbon into a large double bow and use 22-gauge wire to secure it in the middle (see pages 12–15). Make three bows.

7 Push the wire of each bow into the arrangement under a lotus and glue to secure.

8 Hold the wreath against the wall to decide which way up to hang it. Gutter a 22-gauge florist's wire and bend in half to form a hanger (see pages 12–15). Twist the ends of the guttered wire together at the back of the wreath.

Christmas candle table center

For the festive season we have used the traditional colors of red, green, and gold to create a striking candle table center in a burnished gold box. A twisted gold candle gives height, surrounded by green oak leaves and moss, the velvety red of *Celosia*, bright red shiny berries, striking slices of orange, gold-tied cinnamon bundles, and golden seed heads and cones, finished with a sumptuous red and gold ribbon.

Feel the warmth of Christmas, smell the cinnamon and orange, put on a background of carols, slow down and take time to enjoy designing your own holiday table center, to share with family and friends.

Choose your container carefully, to look extravagant but not so much that the Christmas feast is dwarfed, especially on a table where space is limited.

YOU WILL NEED

- **Gold box**
- **Dry florist's foam**
- **Knife**
- **Sphagnum moss**
- **22-gauge 12in (30cm) florist's wire**
- **Candleholder**
- **Twisted gold candle**
- **Green dyed oak leaves**
- **'Hen and Chickens' poppy, sprayed gold**
- **Red *Celosia***
- **Red broom bloom**
- ***Nigella* (green pod), sprayed gold**

- **Twigs, sprayed gold**
- **Artificial red berries**
- **4 orange slices**
- **Cinnamon sticks**
- **Gold cord**
- **Wellingtonia cones, sprayed gold**
- **Glue gun**
- **Dark green reindeer moss**
- **Wide, red and gold ribbon**
- **Scissors**

Gold-sprayed wellingtonia cones, gold-sprayed 'Hen and Chickens' poppies, and orange slices

1 Cut dry florist's foam to fit the box and sit 1in (2.5cm) proud of the top. Fix the foam in place and wedge smaller pieces into the gaps (see pages 12–15).

2 Lightly cover the foam with sphagnum moss and pin (pages 12–15).

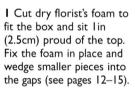

3 Push a candleholder centrally into the foam and insert a gold candle.

4 Push eight to nine small green oak leaves, evenly distributed, into the foam at different angles. Add two groups of two to three gold poppies at either end of the container.

5 Divide red *Celosia* into small florets and double leg wire five small groups (see pages 12–15). Insert them scattered all over. Push in a few pieces of red broom bloom close to the *Celosia*.

6 Add two groups of gold *Nigella* near the poppies, and about four gold twigs close to each *Nigella* group, wildly sticking out of the arrangement. Stand back to check the balance of materials and color.

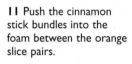

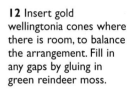

Cerise *Celosia*

7 Pull artificial red berries away from the main stem and wire together in about four groups of three.

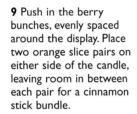

8 Halve four orange slices and wire into pairs (see pages 12–15).

9 Push in the berry bunches, evenly spaced around the display. Place two orange slice pairs on either side of the candle, leaving room in between each pair for a cinnamon stick bundle.

10 Bunch three 4in (10cm) cinnamon sticks together and tie with gold cord. Attach a 22-gauge wire at the back to push into the foam. Make two bundles.

11 Push the cinnamon stick bundles into the foam between the orange slice pairs.

12 Insert gold wellingtonia cones where there is room, to balance the arrangement. Fill in any gaps by gluing in green reindeer moss.

13 Make two single bows of ribbon (see pages 12–15). Wire the bows at either side of the candle and add ribbon tails on the other two sides.

Welcome Christmas visitors with candlelight, held with cinnamon and orange, and displayed to perfection on an oak chest or table.

CHRISTMAS CANDLE TABLE CENTER

TIPS

✿ Keep the material low, well away from the candle flame. Do not let the candle burn unattended, or allow it to burn down to the level of the dried material.

✿ Always remember that, when sitting at a table, your guests will view the arrangement from all angles, so make sure the display looks good from all sides.

Supplier list

NORTH AMERICA

The Flower Mart.com
P.O. Box 1809
Hillsboro, OR   97123
Tel: (503) 628 3167
Fax: (630) 839 7029
or: (503) 628 0647
Web: **www.flowermart.com**
  (No minimum order required)

Dried Flower Shop
Tel: (877) DRIEDFLOWER
or: (877) 374 3335
Web: **www.driedflowershop.com**

Dried Flowers Direct
Keuka Flower Farm
3597 Skyline Dr.
Penn Yan, NY   14527
Tel: (315) 536 2736
Web: **www.driedflowersdirect.com**
Email: **drieds@linkny.com**
  (Minimum order is $25 –
  for any less a processing charge is added)

Michaels Stores Inc.
8000 Bent Branch
Irving, TX   75063
Tel: (800) MICHAELS
or: (800) 642 4235
Web: **www.michaels.com**

Hobby Lobby
Web: **www.hobbylobby.com**

Mac Pherson Enterprises
6 Water St N, Box 1810
St. Marys, ON   N4X-2C1
Canada
Tel: (519) 284 1741

Crafts Canada
2745 29th St. N.E.
Calgary, ON
T1Y-7B5
Tel: (807) 623 3636
Web: **www.crafts-canada.com**
  or: **www.craftscanada.ca**

UNITED KINGDOM

Farmhouse Flora/The Christmas Barn
(Anne Ballard)
Church Farm
Shrawley
Worcester
WR6 6TS
Tel.: (01905) 620283
Fax: (01905) 621608
Email: **information@farmhouseflora.com**
Web: **www.farmhouseflora.com**
Web: **www.thechristmasbarn.com**

British Dried Flower Association
Stonedge
Manor Road
Staverton
Nr. Daventry
Northants
NN11 6JD
Tel/Fax: (01327) 702565
Web: **www.flowergrowers.co.uk**

Coppice Crafts
(Chris Scales)
Blake House
Eastham
Tenbury Wells
Worcester
WR15 8NS
Tel: (01584) 881545

Duo Flowers
(James Smith and Russell Banks)
Unit 10, Beauchamp Business Centre
Sparrowhawk Close
Enigma Business Park
Malvern
WR14 1GL
Tel: (01684) 897770
Fax: (01684) 897780

Twelfth Night
(Berries)
Graham House
Aston Under Hill
Evesham
WR11 6SW
Tel/Fax: (01386) 881239
Web: **www.12thnight.com**

Peter Harvey Floral Art Products
Albany House
Leigh Street
High Wycombe
Bucks
HP11 2QU
Tel: (01494) 533244
Fax: (01494) 443222
Email: **mailbox@pharvey.demon.co.uk**

AUSTRALIA

Deliverers:

Hobart-Flowers.com
Tel: (800) 888351
Fax: (800) 675201
Web: **http://www.hobart-flowers.com**

Fantasy Flowers Florist
Tel: (03) 62341168
Fax: (03) 62313305
Web: **http://www.southcom.com.au/~fantasy**

OzFlorEx
PO Box 341
Armidale NSW 2350
Australia
Tel: (02) 67749200
Fax: (02) 67712610
Web: **http://www.ozflorex.com.au/flowerinfo.htm**

Suppliers:

Kings Herb Seeds
PO Box 975
Penrith NSW 2751
Tel/Fax: (04) 7761493

Bushland Flora
17 Trotman Crescent
Yanchep Lagoon
Yanchep, Western Australia
6035
Tel: (08) 95611636

Index

AUTHOR ACKNOWLEDGMENTS:

I would like to thank the following people, whose help and support was invaluable to the making of this book:

Jackie Fleming for her enormous help and enthusiasm, and Tilda Evans, Caroline Mattock, Sam Routledge, and Kate Mattock for lending me their talents and for their adaptability.

My husband John, Jim Wright, Doug and Ro Gorton, and Duo Flowers for growing and sourcing exquisite materials.

Chris Scales for his nut stick baskets, and Kirstie Ellis for conjuring up the seaboard mirror and silver heart.

Dan, Duncan and Roland Ballard, Nia Bramley, and Charlotte Randall for being scribes and finally James Brookes for his endless talents with the e-mail and patience, and for his ability to make things happen.